Contents

MATRIX
OF
DECEIT

Forcing Pre-Election and Exit Polls to Match Fraudulent Vote Counts

RICHARD CHARNIN

Introduction

The goal of this book is to show the average voter that we have not been told the truth about our elections. As one who has spent a lifetime building computer models in engineering, corporate finance and investment analysis, I am not alone in claiming that our electoral system is broken. But this is not a book about politics. It is about rational and faith-based thinking.

A thorough analysis of the 1988-2008 state and national unadjusted exit polls has revealed startling results which prove systemic election fraud beyond any doubt. The one-sided pattern of "red shift" discrepancies to the recorded vote is mathematically impossible. Informing the average voter of this information is a major focus of this book.

The corporate media and both major political parties are complicit in maintaining the fiction of a democratic system by claiming that the electorate is evenly split between Democrats and Republicans. It's a myth that the media needs to perpetuate in order to make it appear elections are fair. And they accomplish this by manipulating pre-election and exit polls to conform to the recorded vote counts. This practice is nothing new; exit polls have always been forced to match the official counts. Pollsters admit it. The adjustments are growing in magnitude due to the sharp increase in minorities and newly registered Democratic voters – and the growing "red-shift".

One month before the 2012 election, the National Election Pool, a consortium of six media giants which runs the exit polls, decided to eliminate polling in 19 states.

But the 1988-2008 unadjusted exit poll data is an historical fact; systemic election fraud has already been proven. And a post-election analysis of vote share anomalies that are sure to occur in 2012 will be investigated using the True Vote Model which has confirmed the exit polls (and vice-versa) for each of the last six presidential elections.

The Democrats should normally be prohibitive favorites to win the Presidency and Congress. They have captured the majority of new voters in every election since 1988. Obama had better than 72% of new voters; Kerry had approximately 60%. In pre-election polls, the percentage of newly registered Democratic voters is reduced by likely voter cutoff models. Post-election, the exit polls are adjusted to conform to the recorded vote, even if it means assuming an impossible number of voters from the previous election. Polling samples are based on previous recorded votes, not on votes cast. There were 40 million more votes cast than recorded in the last six elections.

In order to have a chance of winning, the Republicans must keep the number of eligible voters as small as possible. They accomplish this though overt voter disenfranchisement. That is Step One. But it's not enough. Step Two is to erase the remaining deficit. This is accomplished covertly by miscounting votes on unverifiable voting machines in which they control the secret code and the vote counting.

The media reports extensively on voter disenfranchisement, but refuse to discuss the fact that private corporations manufacture and control the voting machines and count the votes. This is an ongoing travesty has no place in a democracy. But the Democrats never talk about election fraud at the voting machines.

The scientific method has been ignored by the corporate media. It resorts to disinformation, talking points and faith-based theories on election results. As a result, the true facts about elections are hidden from the public. Historical data, logic and mathematical models are necessary in proving election fraud.

Personal belief and intuition are not enough. One must consider all of the relevant evidence before drawing any conclusions. Unfortunately, a knee-jerk response to new disturbing information is common, especially if it reveals facts outside of an individual's belief system.

Our society depends on mathematics and science, yet the general public is math-phobic and easily fooled by misinformation. If the average person was aware of just a few basic statistical and probability concepts, they would see through the media propaganda. These risk-based concepts are used by voters every day in analyzing alternative purchase, budgeting and investment decisions. This is not rocket science.

Computer-based models that utilize publicly available data and proven mathematical formulas are an absolute requirement for an unbiased election analysis. These include mathematical concepts such as the mean (average), expected value, margin of error, random numbers, probability distributions, sensitivity analysis. It is not necessary to understand mathematical theory or formulas, just the basic concepts

The analysis of elections became possible only recently due to three factors. The personal computer and spreadsheet software have been available since the early 1980s, but it was not until the late 1990s that the Internet became widely available. The three necessary factors were then in place for election analysis.

But just having the technology is not enough. There must be motivation to expend the effort and use the tools to analyze the data. It's safe to say that were it not for the 2000 and 2004 stolen elections, there would have been little or no incentive to uncover systemic fraud.

Chapter 1 discusses the scientific method, logical thinking and introduces probability models. The vast majority of voters are unaware as to the extent of the abuse of the scientific method and the simple mathematics which proves that the final exit polls are bogus.

Chapter 2 reviews the corporate media and academia lockdown on discussion and analysis of election fraud. If these institutions did their job, historical election data would need to be completely revised. The people would realize that they do not live in a true democracy since the votes are not counted as cast.

Chapter 3 covers election forecasting methods and polling simulation models. Pollsters and academics resort to prior election results as a basis for their analysis. Although likely voter (LV) pre-election polls have accurately projected the recorded vote, the question needs to be asked: is forecasting a likely miscounted recorded vote without mentioning the fraud factor legitimate? Or is it in fact providing cover for the fraud?

Chapter 4 is an introduction to exit polling methodology. Adjusted final exit polls misrepresent the actual results. The process of adjusting the exit polls in order to match the recorded vote closes the disinformation loop. Just like the pre-election polls, precincts selected for exit poll samples are largely based on previous election recorded votes – which were also adjusted. And the process continues in every election.

Chapter 5 covers unadjusted state and national exit polls. Of the 274 state presidential exit polls since 1988, 226 (82%) moved in favor of the Republicans in the recorded vote – the so-called "red-shift". Of the 126 polls that exceeded the margin of error, 123 favored the Republicans. A simple calculation shows that if elections were fair, this result would not be possible.

Chapter 6 is an introduction to the True Vote Model. The TVM was developed for post-election analysis and is based on prior and current election votes cast, returning voter turnout and candidate shares of returning and new voters. The True Vote Model and unadjusted exit polls are crucial in proving systemic election fraud because they are unbiased and based on plausible statistics. The 1988, 1992, 2004 and 2008 presidential elections each required an impossible number of returning Bush voters in order to force a match to the recorded vote.

Chapter 7 reviews the 2010 midterm elections. They are represented by the media as a Republican blowout. Pre-election and post election analysis covers senate and gubernatorial elections which appear to be fraudulent.

Chapter 8 is devoted to Wisconsin, which became the focal point of election activism in 2011 as a result of highly suspicious Supreme Court, state senate and governor recall elections. The evidence is compelling that most, if not all, were fraudulent.

Chapter 9 covers the upcoming 2012 presidential election. The pre-election model forecasts the True Vote as well as the official recorded vote. History shows that they always differ. Will Obama be able to overcome the fraud factor?

Chapter 10 reviews the statistical evidence which shows that Oregon has had an excellent record for accurate vote counting since 1998, when it converted to a 100% early voting system of mailed or hand delivered ballots..

Chapter 11 proposes that corrupt, proprietary and unverifiable voting systems be replaced by a combination of hand-counted paper ballots and Open Source software. The Humboldt County, CA open source system photographs and counts the ballots which are stored online for anyone to view. Transparency and data redundancy are paramount.

Chapter 12 reviews some of the election myths and anomalies promoted by the corporate media, academics and online trolls who seek to disrupt discussions related to election integrity.
The Appendix covers basic mathematical concepts and includes 1972-2008 presidential state and national exit polls, true vote models and recorded vote data tables.

My website (*richardcharnin.com*) contains links to my blog and related articles from a wide range of activists. It includes links to online postings dating back to 2004. There are links to state and national exit polls and true vote spreadsheet models. The models were created to analyze the local, state and national elections discussed in this book.

CHAPTER 1

The Age of Unreason

Science is simply common sense at its best - Aldous Huxley

The scientific method is the process of investigating, performing experiments, adding new knowledge or correcting previous information. The method of inquiry is based on "systematic observation, measurement, and experiment, and the formulation, testing, and modification of hypotheses". It is a procedure that has characterized science for nearly four centuries. It seeks to let reality speak for itself, supporting a theory when   predictions are confirmed and challenging it when it is proven to be false.

Scientific researchers propose hypotheses as explanations of systems phenomena, and design experiments to test them. The steps must be repeatable to guard against mistake or confusion in a particular experiment. Theories that encompass other areas of inquiry may bind independently derived hypotheses together in a supportive structure. Theories, in turn, may help form new hypotheses or place groups of hypotheses into context.

Scientific inquiry is generally intended to be as objective as possible in order to reduce biased interpretations of results. Data documents should be archived   for other scientists, so that they can verify the results by attempting to reproduce them. This *full disclosure* allows statistical measures of the reliability of the data to be established. It is sometimes useful to incorporate subjective intuition, experience or expert opinion into a mathematical model.

Logical Thinking

Everyone thinks about problems every day. But how sure are they that their conclusions on how to solve them are valid? This book deals with uncertainty in our election systems. How do we know that the votes are counted as cast? If the information we are given is tainted, how do we know? We must distinguish between intuitive and logical reasoning.

Yet decisions must be made everyday where there are multiple choices. Which make the most sense? Which is the most probable? If you flip a coin and it comes up heads five times in a row, is the next flip more likely to be tails? Is a baseball player with a .300 bating average who has not had a base hit in his last 10 at bats due to get one his next time up? In decision making, we always need to consider probabilities.

In mathematics we need unambiguous definitions and rules. In other words, we need logical thinking. Logic is defined as a systematic study of the conditions and procedures required to make valid inferences.

We start with a statement and infer other statements are valid and justified as a consequence of the initial statement. It is important to note that logical inference does not mean the statement is true, only that it is valid. If the starting statement is true, then a logically derived result must also be true.

For example, it is a statement of fact that Bush had 50.5 million recorded votes in 2000. Approximately 2.5 million Bush 2000 voters died prior to the 2004 election, so there could not have been more than 48 million returning Bush voters. But according to the National Exit poll, there were 52.6 million returning Bush voters. This is clearly impossible.

Furthermore, since the National Exit Poll was adjusted to match the recorded vote, then the recorded vote must also be impossible. This simple deductive reasoning proves 2004 Election Fraud.

The same logic shows that the 1988, 1992 and 2008 elections were also fraudulent; the National Exit Polls were forced to match the recorded vote by indicating there were more returning Bush voters than were alive. The corporate media has never seen fit to explain these recurring impossibilities.

Science is "cumulative". New developments may refine or extend past knowledge. There is no such thing as a foolproof system. What is needed is a probability-based system for many types of problems. It is the only rational way of thinking.

There is no way to eliminate all risk (error) in a system model (or election poll). The problem is to evaluate risk and measure it based on a probability analysis. Every important problem requires a comparison of the odds. Probability analysis supplements classical logical thinking but does not replace it. In fact, classical logic is required in every step in the development of probability theory.

Probability Theory

We are always faced with situations in which we do not have enough information to permit the application of logical thinking. The theory tells us the degree of confidence we can have in coming to a conclusion.

The theory of probability dates back to 17th century France. Mathematicians sought to quantify gambling risk. They determined that the House had a 2.6% advantage (671-635) in the game of dice. In roulette it is 5.26% (38-36).

Probability analysis proves that elections have been fraudulent. Of the 274 state presidential election polls since 1988, 226 moved (the "red-shift") from the exit poll to the vote in favor of the Republican. The odds of this occurrence, assuming the elections were fair, is 1 in 2.7 million trillion trillion.

P =.0000000000 .0000000000 .0000000000037 (3.7E-31)

Of the 274 polls, 126 exceeded the exit poll margin of error. Only 14 would normally be expected. And of the 126 which exceeded the margin of error, 123 favored the Republicans. The probability is effectively absolute ZERO.

Mathematical Models

A model is a description of a system using mathematical equations. Models are used in science, engineering and social science by physicists, engineers, statisticians, operations researchers and economists. A model helps to understand the components of a system and predict future results.

The quality of a scientific field depends on how well models agree with results of repeatable experiments. Comparing a model's output to real world data often leads to the development of new and better theories.

In general, model complexity involves a trade-off between simplicity and accuracy. Given several models with equal predictive power, the simplest one is the most desirable.

Complexity usually improves the realism of a model, but it can make the model difficult to understand and analyze or pose computational problems. As science progresses, explanations tend to become more complex. A paradigm shift based on a radical simplification creates a new theory. Engineers often accept approximations in order to get a more robust and simple model.

Mathematical models express system variables in the form of equations (functions). A deterministic model is one in which variables are determined by parameters in the model and performs the same way for a given set of initial conditions. Conversely, in a stochastic model, variables are described by probability distributions – as in forecasting the electoral vote.

A crucial part of the modeling process is to determine if a mathematical model describes a system accurately using several methods of evaluation. The easiest part is checking whether the model fits experimental measurements or other empirical data.

One approach is to test the model by splitting the data into two data subsets: training and verification. Training data are used to estimate the model's structure using mathematical equations

Verification data is used to test the accuracy of the model even though the data was not used in its development. Measuring (verification) discrepancies between observed and predicted data is a useful tool in assessing the accuracy of a model and to determine the possible cause of the discrepancies – as in polling.

A model's scope is represented by those systems for which it is applicable. If the model is constructed based on a set of data, one must determine the systems or situations for which the data is applicable. For example, the True Vote Model, partially based on exit polling, has applicability in local, state and national elections.

A static model does not account for the element of time (such as polling data on a given date). Dynamic models, such as the Recursive True Vote Model and pre-election forecasting models based on historical time-series data.

A deductive model is a logical structure based on a theory. An inductive model is based empirical results of experiments and generalization from them.

A black-box model is a system for which no prior information is available. Usually it is preferable to use as much prior information as possible to improve a model's accuracy - as long as the information is relevant.

The model should not engage in "overkill" by including extraneous variables which do not add to its accuracy - and in fact, may contaminate, the results. For example, the contamination of "pristine" exit poll results with recorded vote counts.

CHAPTER 2

Media Misinformation

It is difficult to get a man to understand something, when his salary depends on his not understanding it - Upton Sinclair

Historical facts and data are either unstated or misrepresented by the media. Pundits and exit pollsters have consistently used one argument to explain the massive exit poll discrepancies are one-sided in favor of the Republicans: **Democratic voters are more responsive to the exit pollsters than Republican voters.**

The constant rehashing of the so-called reluctant Bush responder theory (rBr) has been the primary propaganda technique used to fool the average voter. It has no basis in fact.

The "experts" provide no other explanation and have not presented any evidence to back up the claim. It's a myth, pure and simple. In fact, if the pundits did their homework, they would find that in each of the 2000, 2004 and 2008 presidential elections, exit poll response rates were highest in Republican strongholds.

Recorded votes have deviated sharply from the unadjusted exit polls (and the true vote) in every election since 1968. On the other hand, unadjusted exit polls have always been accurate and have closely matched the True Vote Model in each of the 1988-2008 elections.

Internet Conspiracy Bloggers

Published state and national exit polls have exactly matched the recorded vote because they have been forced to do so. It is standard policy. But the recorded vote has never reflected true voter intent due to uncounted ballots and maliciously programmed electronic voting machines.

Statistical analyses provided by Internet bloggers concluded that Bush stole the 2004 election. Their findings were dismissed by the media as "just another conspiracy theory".

A few "conspiracy fraudsters" were banned after posting on various liberal discussion forums. And even today, the most popular polling sites never discuss election fraud.

But the Democrats haven't raised the issue after two presidential and scores of congressional and gubernatorial elections were stolen. Neither has the media, supposedly the guardians of democracy. Is there anyone who still truly believes that elections are legitimate?

In the 1988-2008 presidential elections, 126 of 274 state exit polls exceeded the margin of error – and 123 red-shifted to the Republican. Dos the pundits have any idea what the probability is? At the 95% confidence level, 14 of the 274 exit polls would be expected to exceed the margin of error (7 for the Democrat and 7 for the Republican).

Pundits refuse to accept the mathematics which proves that Election Fraud is systemic. It is 2012, and they still want to fool the public into believing the recorded vote accurately depicts the vote count – and that the exit polls are always wrong.

The factual evidence shows that in 1988-2008 presidential elections, the Democrats won the average unadjusted state exit poll aggregate by a massive 52-42% margin. The official recorded vote margin was 48-46%. The independent True Vote Model (described later in the book) confirmed the exit polls.

Proof of systematic vote miscounts is simple and self-explanatory. According to the US Census, there were 80 million more votes cast then recorded in the 1968-2008 presidential elections. The uncounted votes were a combination of spoiled, provisional and absentee ballots. The vast majority were, not surprisingly, Democratic. That fact by itself proves that the recorded vote has never represented the will of the electorate.

Historical election results are reported by the corporate media without consideration of uncounted and miscounted votes. Media pundits and political scientists persist in accepting the unscientific, faith-based practice of adjusting (forcing) the exit polls to match the recorded votes - even when the adjustments are mathematically impossible. Election forecasters and political scientists implicitly assume that the recorded vote is equal to the True Vote. They never consider systemic Election Fraud.

Media Myths

The media still claims that the average final 2004 pre-election polls predicted a Bush win. But they don't tell you that the weighted average predicted Kerry. Or that they were based on LV polls before allocating undecided voters. RV polls, adjusted for undecided voters, predicted a 51-48% Kerry win or that Kerry won 57-62% of new voters.

Another myth is that exit polls were accurate in elections prior to 2004. But state and national exit polls published in the media have always been forced to match the recorded vote, so they only *appear* to have been accurate. Comparing final exit polls prior to 2004 to unadjusted exit polls since is like apples to oranges.

Prior to 2004, uncounted ballots in heavily Democratic districts were a primary cause of the exit poll discrepancies. But in 2002 the Help America Vote Act (HAVA) resulted in the installation of thousands of unverifiable, proprietary voting machines that were vulnerable to computer hacking and malicious coding.

The experts fail to account for the election fraud factor in their historical analyses and polling models. They promote overly complex or simplistic pre-election and post election models but avoid the scientific method and a rational probability and statistical analysis.

The pundits claim that likely voter (LV) pre-election polls have been very accurate in matching the recorded vote. That is true, but they don't mention that the votes are miscounted in every election.

Neither do they mention that their predictions failed to include the majority of newly registered Democratic voters who did not pass the Likely Voter Cutoff Model (LVCM) screen but who actually voted.

They claim that registered voter polls (RV) don't reflect actual voter turnout. That is only partially true; not all registered voters turn out. But they don't tell you that predictions based on RV polls (after allocating undecided voters) closely matched the unadjusted exit polls in 2004, 2006 and 2008. Or that spoiled and uncounted ballots reduce the actual number of votes cast, making it appear that turnout to be lower than it actually was.

The pundits don't mention that over 80 million votes (mostly Democratic) were uncounted in the 11 elections since 1968. In 1988, 11 million uncounted ballots may have cost Dukakis the election. Did the media ever mention it? They are silent about the six million uncounted votes in 2000.

They never consider the overwhelming evidence that the 2000 and 2004 elections were stolen and that Democratic landslides were denied in 2006 and 2008. Or that Senate and Governor elections were likely stolen in 2010.

They ignore the massive statistical evidence which confirms Election Fraud, yet never stop talking about non-existent voter fraud. They discuss overt disenfranchisement of voters as if voter suppression is the only problem that needs to be addressed.

But the real problem is miscounting votes cast at the polling site. The media won't talk about covert election fraud at the voting machines. Why they won't is the single biggest "tell" of all.

They refer to the final exit polls to analyze demographic trends. But they don't tell you that the final exit polls are always forced to match the recorded vote – and therefore all demographic category crosstabs understate the true Democratic share.

Another media myth is that the 2000 election was close and that Gore won by 540,000 recorded votes. The Florida recount was halted by the Supreme Court. But a total count of all the ballots after the election showed that more than 185,000 were spoiled and uncounted. Bush won by 537 votes.

Gore's name was punched on 75% of the 113,000 that were double and triple punched. He lost thousands of votes in Palm Beach County due to the infamous "butterfly" ballots, when voters who meant to vote for him were fooled by a confusing allot design into voting for Buchanan.

The media never reported that Gore won the Florida exit poll by 53.4-43.6% or that he won the National Exit Poll by 48.5-46.3% and the state exit polls by 50.8-45.5%, a 6 million vote margin.

Reluctant Republican Responders

The following selected paragraphs are from Chapter 1 in the newly released text, *Exit Polls: Surveying the American Electorate, 1972-2010* by Samuel J. Best, University of Connecticut and Brian S. Krueger, University of Rhode Island.

"VRS claimed the Democratic overstatement in the raw exit poll data was due to partisan differences in the willingness of voters to complete the exit poll, not to a poor selection of precincts or differential response rates by age, race, or gender. Republicans simply refused to participate at the same rates as Democrats, resulting in there being fewer Republicans in the raw exit poll results than there should have been.

Mitofsky speculated that the disparity was due to different intensities of support for the candidates – Democratic voters were just more excited about voting for Clinton than Republican voters were about voting for Bush and, as a result, were more motivated to communicate this message by filling out the exit poll questionnaire; others thought it was due to Republicans in general having less confidence in the mass media."

The authors fail to mention that one very plausible reason the exit polls were "off" in 1992 was the fact that nearly 10 million ballots were never counted, the majority from minority precincts that were heavily Democratic. These voters were exit polled, but their votes were not counted. There were 11 million uncounted ballots in 1988, 9 million in 1996, 6 million in 2000 and 4 million in 2004.

According to investigative reporter Greg Palast, approximately 4 million were uncounted in 2008.

There is no evidence that Democrats were more responsive. In fact, in each of the 2000, 2004 and 2008 elections, average response rates in GOP strongholds were higher than Democratic strongholds. GOP exit poll and vote shares were positively correlated (.25) to state exit poll response. Bush vote shares increased as response rates increased. The average Democratic correlation was of course, just the opposite: -0.26. In 2004, precinct data showed that response rates were higher in partisan Bush precincts.

"Despite the source of the partisan bias in the raw results, the exit polls were able to characterize accurately the voting patterns of demographic subgroups and partisan constituencies once they were weighted to match the official returns. The problem was that the data could not be corrected until the official results began coming in. As a result, the exit polls were susceptible to inaccurate vote projections on election night, especially early in the evening right after poll closings. Nonetheless, the cautious analysts at VRS still called all the races correctly in the 1992 election."

The data could not be corrected until the official votes came in? Or was it that the data could not be *rigged* until they came in? Of course the cautious analysts called the winner. But Clinton won a major landslide by a much higher margin than the analysts anticipated.

"Network competition to call winners culminated in the disastrous 2000 presidential election, when these systems of race projections broke down, and the networks wound up retracting their calls for the winner in Florida and presumptively the election, not once, but twice on election night. The trouble began early in the evening, when VNS alerted the networks around 7:50 p.m. that their statistical models predicted Al Gore the winner in Florida and that the networks should consider calling the state for Gore. This prediction took place even though only 4 percent of the actual vote had been counted and numerous precincts in the Florida panhandle, which happened to be in the central time zone, remained open until 8 p.m."

If the exit polls show a clear winner - as they did in Florida - the fact that just 4% of the votes were recorded is irrelevant. The exit polls were completed by 7:50pm – and panhandle precincts were exit polled throughout the day.

Calling the race 10 minutes before the polls closed was of no consequence. Gore won the Florida exit poll (1816 respondents) by a whopping 53.4-43.6%, far beyond the 3% margin of error.

Of the 185,000 spoiled ballots in Florida, 113,000 were double and triple punched – and Gore's name was punched on 75% of them. Almost 30,000 over-punched ballots were in Duval County which has a large black population. Could the spoiled ballots have been the cause of the Duval adjustments?

Impossible Bush 2000 Voter Turnout in 2004

They claim that Bush won by 3 million votes. But they won't tell you that to match the recorded vote, the Final 2004 National Exit Poll (NEP) required 6 million more returning Bush 2000 voters than were alive in 2004 - a mathematically impossible 110% turnout.

The adjusted National Exit Poll indicated that there were 52.6 million returning Bush 2000 voters. But he had just 50.5 million recorded votes in 2000. There had to be 110% turnout of living Bush 2000 voters in order to match the 2004 recorded vote – obviously a physical and mathematical impossibility which also occurred in 1972, 1988, 1992 and 2008 for the Republican candidate.

In 2004, preliminary state exit poll numbers were downloaded from the CNN website by Jonathan Simon. Kerry led by 50-48%.

The state polls were already in the process of being matched to the recorded vote. But Bush was winning the vote count – a massive divergence from the exit polls. We later learned that Kerry led the National Exit Poll from 4pm to midnight buy a steady 51-48%. . But we didn't see the numbers. They were not meant for public viewing.

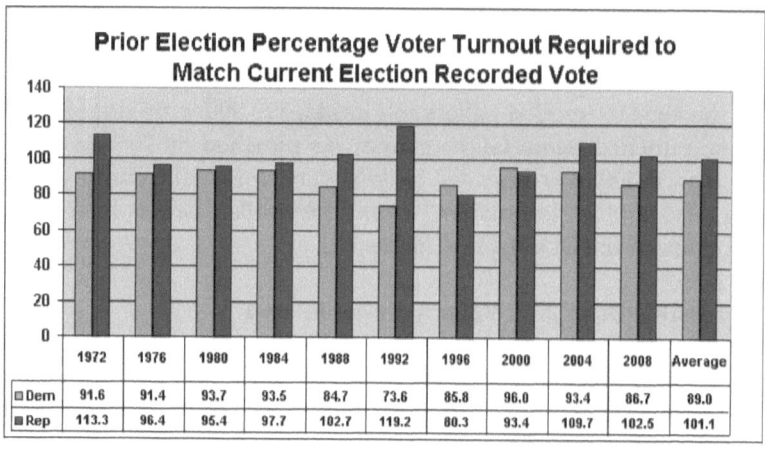

Prior Election Percentage Voter Turnout Required to Match Current Election Recorded Vote

	1972	1976	1980	1984	1988	1992	1996	2000	2004	2008	Average
Dem	91.6	91.4	93.7	93.5	84.7	73.6	85.8	96.0	93.4	86.7	89.0
Rep	113.3	96.4	95.4	97.7	102.7	119.2	80.3	93.4	109.7	102.5	101.1

"Considering the closeness of the election, the exit polls seemed to suggest that Kerry was capable of winning the 2004 election. Political observers used these differences between the preliminary exit polls and the final results to support allegations of vote rigging and fraud in precincts deploying electronic voting machines, particularly in Ohio, where the state's twenty-seven electoral votes, enough to change the winner of the Electoral College from Bush to Kerry, was decided by 118,775 ballots."

CNN and NYT websites showed that Bush won the National Exit Poll (13,660 respondents) by 51-48% – matching the recorded vote.

How did 613 National Exit Poll respondents enable Bush to flip the vote? The exit pollsters never could answer that one. It was mathematically impossible. The unadjusted 2004 exit poll proved it, but was not released until long after the damage was done.

"Edison-Mitofsky also found that voting patterns within electoral groups were accurate once they were weighted to the official results. They found no evidence that the distribution of presidential vote choices within various demographic groups was biased, despite the vote choice of exit poll respondents overall overstating Democratic support."

The unadjusted polls show that Kerry actually won the majority of the 13,660 respondents 51.7- 46.9%. But the unadjusted National Exit Poll was "not meant for public viewing". It showed that returning Gore voters comprised 38.4% of the electorate and Bush voters 39.5%, suggesting that the poll may have been biased for Bush since Gore won the recorded vote by 0.5%.

Another major anomaly: *The adjusted final exit poll was forced to match the recorded vote with an impossible 110% turnout of living Bush 2000 voters.*

Vote shares are calculated the same way for all exit poll categories (crosstabs). The weight is multiplied by the corresponding vote share. The total share is the sum of the weighted shares.

2004 National Exit Poll				2004 How Voted in 2000 (weighted to Bush)				
Sample	Kerry	Bush	Other	Sample	DNV	Gore	Bush	Other
13,660	7,064	6,414	182	3,182	585	1,221	1,257	119
	51.7%	46.9%	1.3%	-	18.4%	38.4%	39.5%	3.7%

Unadjusted National Exit Poll					Adjusted National Exit Poll (recorded)				
2000	Mix	Kerry	Bush	Other	Mix	Kerry	Bush	Other	Turnout
DNV	18.4%	57%	41%	2%	17%	54%	44%	2%	-
Gore	38.4%	91%	8%	1%	37%	90%	10%	0%	93%
Bush	39.5%	10%	90%	0%	43%	9%	91%	0%	110%
Other	3.7%	64%	17%	19%	3%	64%	14%	22%	98%
Total	100%	51.7%	46.8%	1.5%	100%	48.3%	50.7%	1.0%	
Votes	125.7	65.1	58.8	1.84	122.3	59.0	62.0	1.2	

Kerry's total vote share is a simple calculation:
$51.7\% = .184^*.57 + .384^*.91 + .395^*.10 + .037^*.64$

One week after the 2004 election, MSNBC's Keith Olbermann presented a powerful expose of the nefarious election anomalies in Ohio and Florida. The election was stolen, not just from Kerry, but from the 67 million who voted for him. Olbermann never followed up on the massive election fraud. Once again, the public was hoodwinked by the corporate media into believing that Bush won by 3 million votes. But Kerry won the True Vote in a 10 million landslide.

Edison-Mitofsky claimed that the selected precinct sample was near-perfect, yet they ignored the fact that there were nearly six million uncounted votes in 2000. In Florida, 185,000 spoiled punch card ballots were never counted – and 70% were for Gore. GOP election officials discarded Democratic absentee ballots and included GOP ballots filed after the due date. And of course, there was the infamous butterfly ballot. Gore won Florida easily.

"Exit polls may also miss late voters. By "late" voters they mean persons who come to their polling place in the last couple of hours of the day, after the exit polls are out of the field. Although there is no clear consensus about which types of voters tend to vote later rather than earlier, this adds another way in which the sample may be nonrandom, particularly in precincts with long lines or extended voting hours... a high-turnout election may make demographic weighting difficult".

In the 2006 midterms, the Democrats won the House by 52-46% (230-205 seats). They won all 120 pre-election Generic Polls. The trend line predicted a 56.4% share - exactly matching the unadjusted National Exit Poll. Approximately 20 House seats were stolen (primarily in FL, OH, NM and IL). The landslide was denied.

"National exit pollsters account for early/absentee voting by conducting telephone surveys in states where the rates of early voting are highest. VNS first incorporated early/absentee voting in 1996, surveying voters in California, Oregon, Texas, and Washington. By 2008, NEP was conducting telephone surveys in eighteen states, including Oregon, Washington, and Colorado, where the proportions of early voting were so high that no in-person exit polls were conducted on Election Day".

Early voting results in 2008 election shows that Oregon, Washington, and Colorado had the lowest exit poll discrepancies. Was it just a coincidence that the states with the highest early voting rates closely matched the unadjusted exit polls?

Sample Precincts based on Prior Election Recorded Votes

"Within each of these size strata, precincts are categorized by geographic region, usually between three to five regions in each state. For each state geographic region, precincts are ordered by their percentage vote for one of the major political parties in a previous election. Precincts are sampled from these strata with probabilities proportionate to the total votes cast in them in a prior election, so that every precinct has as many chances of being picked by pollsters as it has voters. The samples drawn in each state are then combined, and a national sample of precincts is selected from them using a previous presidential race to determine the relative number of precincts chosen from each state."

"Overstatement repeatedly found in the national exit polls over the past several decades appears to be due to the greater willingness of Democratic voters to complete the exit polls, compared with their Republican counterparts. However, once this discrepancy has been corrected by weighting the exit polls to correspond with the actual vote, there has been no evidence that the vote estimates within groups are biased".

Sampling voters in proportion to the recorded vote in prior elections is a persistent source of bias, since the recorded votes were fraudulent and favored the Republicans. So the sampled exit polled precincts were over-weighted for the GOP.

Democratic greater willingness to be exit polled than Republicans is a myth. In fact, the exit poll data shows otherwise. In 2000, 2004 and 2008, Republican exit poll and vote shares were positively correlated (.25) to state exit poll response. In 2004, Bush vote shares increased as response rates increased, refuting the Reluctant Republican Responder hypothesis. The "overstating" of 56 Kerry respondents for every 50 Bush respondents was not due to differential response; it was due to the fact that Kerry won the election with 53% of the vote.

"Since 2004, less controversy has surrounded the exit polls. No serious technical problems have surfaced during the last three elections, enabling the media to prepare analyses of the outcome in a timely manner. Leaks of early wave findings have been contained. The preliminary exit polls have continued to overstate support for Democratic candidates; however, the final vote counts have had such large winning margins that the projected outcomes were no different."

The pundits claim that the pre-election LV polls predicted Obama's 52.9-45.6% recorded share. They are correct; LV polls are usually quite accurate when it comes to predicting the recorded vote. But RV polls projected that he would win by 57-41%.

There was no controversy as in 2000 and 2004, but only because Obama won by 9.5 million recorded votes (52.9-45.6%). The level of fraud was greater than 2004.

Conspiracy of Silence

Obama won the unadjusted National Exit Poll by 61-37%. The pundits never discuss this that Obama's exit poll margin was reduced from 17% to 7.5% by fraud. The state exit polls indicated that he won by nearly 23 million with a 58.0% share. The landslide was denied.

The NEP indicated there were 5 million returning third party voters. But only 1.2 million were recorded in 2004. Either the NEP or the 2000 vote count (or both) was incorrect. Neither the pollsters nor the media has ever mentioned that in order to match the recorded vote, the adjusted National Exit Poll required 12 million more returning 2004 Bush than Kerry voters - an impossible 103% turnout of living Bush voters.

They fail to question the 2010 midterms. The Democrats easily won the unadjusted Governor exit polls in Florida and Ohio but lost both elections. Giannoulias won the Illinois Senate exit poll and lost. So did Sestak in Pennsylvania.

Nate Silver, a blogger at the New York Times, wrote that there were ten reasons why we should not believe the exit polls. Did he mean the final, adjusted polls or the unadjusted polls "not meant for public viewing"?

If he meant the final adjusted exit polls, then he must believe election fraud is systemic since the finals are always forced to match the recorded vote - even if the election is fraudulent. If he meant the unadjusted exit polls, then he must believe that election fraud is a myth. Silver's comments follow in italics.

"Exit polls have a much larger intrinsic margin for error than regular polls. This is because of what are known as cluster sampling techniques. Exit polls are not conducted at all precincts, but only at some fraction thereof. Although these precincts are selected at random and are supposed to be reflective of their states as a whole, this introduces another opportunity for error to occur (say, for instance, that a particular precinct has been canvassed especially heavily by one of the /campaigns). This makes the margins for error somewhere between 50-90% higher than they would be for comparable telephone surveys."

But exit polls have a much smaller margin of error than pre-election polls. That is a given. Even Dick Morris agrees. Exit pollsters Edison-Mitofsky state that respondents were randomly-selected and the overall margin of error was 1% in both the notes to the National Exit Poll notes and in the NEP Methods Statement.

It stands to reason that exit polls are more accurate because a) those respondents know exactly who they voted for and b) in pre-election polls, respondents might change their mind – or not vote. The naysayers need to distinguish between the bogus recorded vote that they use in all of their analysis and the True Vote (which they never discuss. The pollsters and the media believe there no such thing as Election Fraud. They ignore the simple identity:

Recorded Vote = True Vote + Election Fraud factor

"Exit polls have consistently overstated the Democratic share of the vote and cite the 2004 election, when leaked exit polls suggested that John Kerry would have a much better day than he actually had. In 2000, for instance, exit polls had Al Gore winning states like Alabama and Georgia."

Of course the Democrats always do better in the exit polls than in the recorded vote. But the naysayers never consider one obvious reason: uncounted votes. The U.S. Census reported that there have been approximately 80 million net uncounted votes since 1968. The vast majority were Democratic (50% are in minority districts).

Exit poll naysayers assume the recorded vote represents the True Vote. Uncounted votes alone debunk that argument. Not to mention votes switched at DREs and central tabulators. A linear regression analysis showed that nonresponse rates increased going from RED states to BLUE states.

Nate cites the 2008 primaries, claiming *"the polls were particularly bad since they overstated Barack Obama's performance by an average of about 7 points."*

But he failed to consider election fraud. He ignores the fact that Obama led in all New Hampshire pre-election polls and the fact that Rush Limbaugh called for an "Operation Chaos". He advised Republicans to cross over in the Democratic primaries and vote for Hillary Clinton. Nate also ignored the fact that Obama easily won all of the caucuses – which could not be rigged.

"Exit polls challenge the definition of a random sample. Although the exit polls have theoretically established procedures to collect a random sample – essentially, having the interviewer approach every nth person who leaves the polling place - in practice this is hard to execute at a busy polling place, particularly when the pollster may be standing many yards away from the polling place itself because of electioneering laws."

Standing "many yards away"? Exit pollsters Edison-Mitofsky state that voters were randomly selected as they exit the polling booth.

Nate repeats a classic canard, citing GOP pollster Rasmussen as *"having found that Democrats supporters are more likely to agree to participate in exit polls, probably because they are more enthusiastic about this election."*

There is no evidence that Democrats are more likely to participate. In fact, 2000, 2004 and 2008 state exit poll response shows just the opposite. The reluctant Bush responder (rBr) canard was debunked by the exit pollster's categorized precinct vote data into five partisan grouping in their 2004 report: High Bush, Bush, Even, Kerry, High Kerry

"Exit polls may have problems calibrating results from early voting. Contrary to the conventional wisdom, exit polls will attempt to account for people who voted before Election Day in most (although not all) states by means of a random telephone sample of such voters. However, this requires the polling firms to guess at the ratio of early voters to regular ones, and sometimes they do not guess correctly.

In Florida in 2000, for instance, there was a significant underestimation of the absentee vote, which that year was a substantially Republican vote, leading to an overestimation of Al Gore's share of the vote, and contributing to the infamous miscall of the state".

But in 2008 the three states with the highest percentage of early voters (Oregon, Washington and Colorado) also had the lowest exit poll discrepancies.

"Exit polls are really more trouble than they are worth, at least as a predictive tool."

But what about using exit polls as a forensic tool? The purpose of an exit poll is to tell us how people in various demographic categories voted. That it also happens to show that Democrats always do better in the polls than the recorded vote is icing on the cake.

Secretary of State Hillary Rodham Clinton criticized Russia for a parliamentary election she claimed was rigged. She also said that election gains by Islamist parties must not set back Egypt's push toward democracy. Hillary talked about Election Fraud in Russia. But we never hear a peep from politicians or the media about systemic election fraud in the U.S. The hypocrisy is overwhelming.

Cenk Uygur is a hard-hitting progressive blogger who hosts *The Young Turks* on Current TV. His boss is Al Gore, the man who was elected president in 2000 but never took office. Cenk covered the 2012 NH primary and the subject of exit polls came up. Guests Al Goreand Jennifer Granholm immediately reverted to the media canard that the polls are not reliable. Quite strange.

Al Gore knows that he won in 2000 and the exit polls indicated just that. In Florida 16,000 votes were deducted from Gore's total in Volusia county. Fox News called Florida for Bush and the other networks immediately did likewise. Al Gore knows that exit polls are accurate; his comment was a real letdown.

Perhaps Cenk will at some point discuss the hypocrisy of politicians and media pundits who criticize election fraud outside the U.S. but never discuss it here.

CHAPTER 3

Forecasting Models

If the facts don't fit the theory, change the facts - Albert Einstein

Pollsters are paid to predict the recorded vote – not the True Vote. They typically use regression models based on historical time-series that are executed months before the election. On the other hand, projections based on state and national polling trends which forecast the popular and electoral vote are updated frequently right up to the election.

In every presidential election, millions of voters are disenfranchised and millions of votes are uncounted. All forecasting models should have the following disclaimer:

Note: this recorded vote forecast will surely deviate from the exit polls. If they are nearly equal, then there must have been errors in one or more of the following: a) input data, b) the assumptions, c) model logic or d) methodology.

The historical evidence is clear: state and national likely voter pre-election polls (adjusted for undecided voters) are superior to time-series models executed months in advance. The forecast models assume that elections will be fraud-free. But they never are. *And that is why this book was written.*

Forecasters avoid the election fraud factor. They never consider that the recorded vote always differs from the true vote – and that votes are miscounted in every election. The implicit assumption is that the official recorded vote will accurately reflect the True Vote and that the election will be fraud-free.

Models which predicted a Bush win in 2000 and 2004 were technically "correct"; he won the *recorded vote*. But the recorded vote is never the same as the *True Vote*. Gore and Kerry each won the True Vote.

Election models executed 2-9 months before the 2004 election forecast that Bush would win the 2-party popular vote with an average 53.9% share. He had 51.2% recorded, but just 47.5%

according to the aggregate unadjusted state exit polls. Furthermore, the corresponding popular vote win probabilities were incompatible with the forecast shares. Not one of the models forecast the electoral vote. Not one mentioned the possibility of election fraud.

There has been much misinformation regarding electoral and popular vote win probability calculations. In the Election Model, the latest state pre-election polls are used to project the vote after adjusting for undecided voters. The model assumes the election is held on the day of the projection.

Academics and political scientists create multiple regression forecasting models which utilize time-series data as relevant input variables: economic growth, inflation, job growth, interest rates, foreign policy, historical election vote shares, etc. Regression modeling is an interesting theoretical exercise but does not account for the daily events which affect voter psychology. Fraud could conceivably skew regression models and media tracking polls.

Polling and regression models are analogous to the market value of a stock and its intrinsic (theoretical) value. The latest poll share is the equivalent of the current stock price. The intrinsic value of a stock is based on forecast cash flows. The intrinsic value is rarely equal to the market value.

Election blogs, media pundits and academics develop models for forecasting the recorded vote. They create overly simple or complex models but avoid forecasting the electoral vote and corresponding win probabilities - or do so incorrectly.

Prominent election forecasters discuss their methodologies in the International Journal of Forecasting. They range from descriptions of diverse forecasting models, such as political futures markets and historical economic time series, to a set of key criteria measures. But none dare mention the *election fraud factor*. If they did, they would undermine the "democracy" myth. Examples of forecasting model factors include:

a) Second-quarter growth rate in the gross domestic product and results of the trial-heat (preference) Gallup poll near Labor Day.

b) Primary vote forecasts in contests where the incumbent president was not a candidate.

c) Forecasts for the in-party candidate based on presidential approval in June.

d) Economic growth in the first half of the election year and whether the president's party is seeking more than a second consecutive term in office.

e) Preferred economic measure and optimal time to issue a forecast.

f) GNP growth and presidential popularity vs. jobs.

g) Bayesian Model averaging to determine if economic influences have an impact on elections without an incumbent candidate.

h) Trial-heat and economic forecasting model.

i) Iowa Electronic Market (IEM).

j) Thirteen key questions about how the president's party has been doing and the circumstances surrounding the election.

Statistical analyses provided by Internet bloggers concluded that Bush stole the 2004 election. Their findings were dismissed by the media as "just another conspiracy theory". A number of them, including this writer, were banned after posting on various discussion forums.

And even today, most popular political websites, along with the mainstream media, never mention election fraud. There have been exceptions, such as Victoria Colliers Oct. 2012 article in Harper's and the June 2006 Robert f. Kennedy Jr. piece in Rolling Stone Magazine. But the media and the Democrats remain silent, even after two presidential and scores of congressional and gubernatorial elections were stolen. Is there anyone who still truly believes that elections are legitimate?

For example, Bush's approval rating was highly correlated and consistently 2-3% higher) to his pre-election poll share. But the media never questioned why his final 50.7% share would be 2.2% higher than his 48.5% approval rating and 3.8% higher than his final National Poll share.

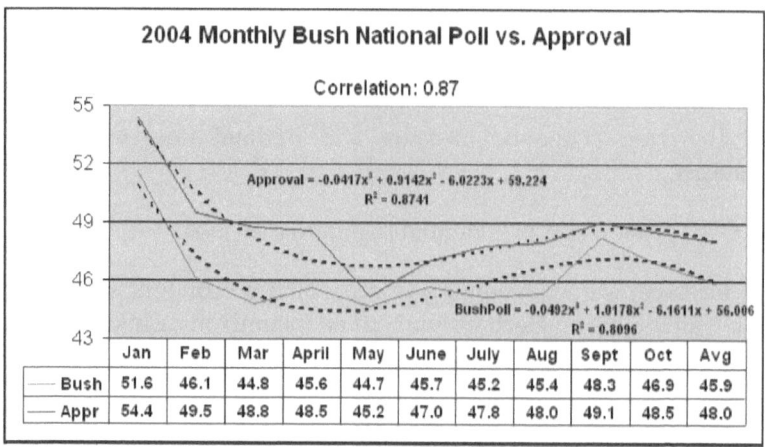

In every election since 1976 in which the incumbent had an approval rating below 50%, he lost his bid for re-election- except for Bush in 2004.

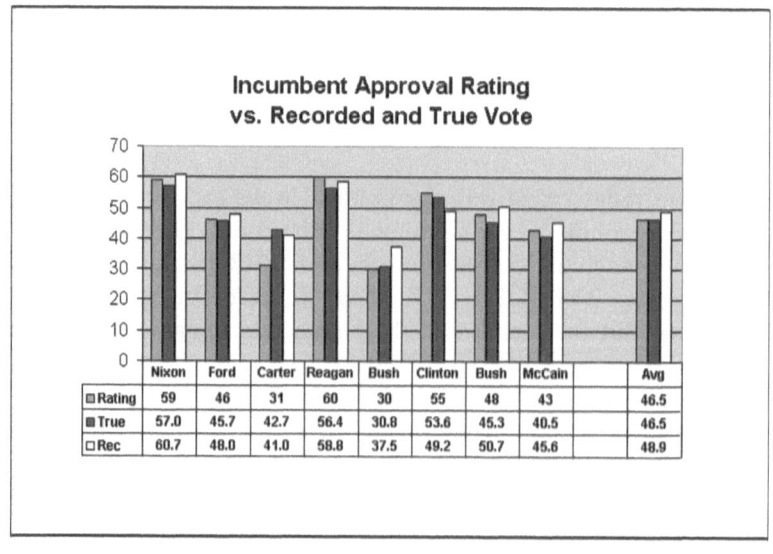

Overview of Sampling Theory

A random sample is one in which each outcome has an equal probability of being included. It is an unbiased estimate of the characteristics of the population in which respondents are theoretically representative of the population as a whole.

Reliability of the sample increases with the sample-size. A random sample of 1,000 will be accurate to within 3 percentage points (the margin of error) 95% of the time (the confidence level). For example, if a random sample of 1,000 shows that 60 percent favor candidate X, there is a 95 percent chance that the real figure in the population is the range from 57 to 63 percent.

The Law of Large Numbers is the basis for statistical sampling. All things being equal, polling accuracy is directly related to sample size – the larger the sample, the smaller the margin of error (Margin of error). In an unbiased random sample, there is a 95% probability that the vote will fall within the Margin of error.

Beyond a certain point, size of the population makes little difference. The confidence interval is not reduced dramatically. Pre-election national polls usually don't exceed 1,500 respondents. Increasing the number will increase the cost of the survey almost proportionately, but the margin of error will only decrease slightly.

It is often not practical to carry out a pure random sample. In an area cluster sample, a number of Primary Sampling Units (PSUs) are selected at random within a larger geographic area. For example, a study of the United States might begin by choosing a subset of congressional districts. Within each PSU, smaller areas may be selected in several stages down to the individual household. Within each household, an individual respondent is then chosen. Ideally, each stage of the process is carried out at random. The sampling error will tend to be higher than in a pure random sample, but the cost savings makes the trade-off well worthwhile.

A stratified sample is appropriate when it is important to ensure inclusion in the sample of sufficient numbers of respondents within subcategories of the population. Strict random sampling is a goal that can almost never be fully achieved under real world conditions since it results in non-random ("systematic") error. For example, assume a survey is being conducted by phone. Not everyone has one or is home when called. People may refuse to participate. The resulting sample willing and able to participate may differ from other potential respondents.

Apart from non-randomness of samples, there are other sources of systematic error in surveys. Slight differences in question wording may produce large differences in how questions are answered. The order in which questions are asked may influence responses. Respondents may lie.

Clinton's 1996 margin

In the March 1997 *Public Perspective* article *"Why Most Polls Overestimated the Clinton Margin"*, Humphrey Taylor suggested that four sources of forecasting "error" (differential polling response, late vote swing, differential voter turnout and polling effect) were all working in 1996.

Taylor did not consider vote miscounts or that there were nearly 10 million more ballots cast than recorded. Clinton defeated Dole by 49.2-40.7%, an 8.5% margin. The final polls had him up by 13-16%. The unadjusted state exit poll aggregate confirmed the pre-election polls; he led by 52.6-37.1%, a 15.5% margin.

Taylor wrote that pre-election polls operate on the assumption that with some weighting, the eligible voters surveyed are representative of the total population, but that in presidential elections, the exit polls do not have to be concerned with late swing or differential response. Yet they appear to *"slightly overstate Democratic and understate Republican votes"*.

He cited the hypothesis that Republicans are "hostile" to the supposed "liberal" press and do not respond to the pollsters.

But he also states that the differential response effect (later called the reluctant Republican responder) is contradicted by the British elections. Extensive studies show that conservative Tories are more likely to be polled.

The "late swing" effect was Clinton's lead diminished between September and Election Day. The Harris Poll had his 21% lead decline to 16%. In the Gallup Nov.2-3 poll, Clinton led by 16%, which declined to 13% in the final pre-election poll.

He also cites the final Harris poll which showed Dole supporters more likely to vote than Clinton's as evidence of the differential turnout effect. But even if true, it does not negate the final likely voter polls which showed Clinton winning by 13-14%

The "poll effect" was based on the hypothesis that the large Clinton lead damaged Dole's chances of winning, but the effect cannot be measured. The discrepancy between Clinton's projected pre-election share and the recorded vote apparently debunked the so-called "bandwagon effect". The author suggests that the Harris poll supported the theory that the "poll effect" caused more Clinton than Dole voters to stay home.

Taylor suggests that the four factors contributed to the nearly 7% "overstatement" in Clinton's margin. Even though the article was written in 1997, the same arguments are still used today (especially differential response) despite the fact that the response data shows Republicans respond at a higher rate than Democrats, just like Tories respond at a higher rate than Labor in Britain.

Journalists who use polls to measure the "horse race" aspect of a political campaign face additional problems. One is guessing the number of respondents who will turn out to vote.

Likely Voter Cutoff Models

Most pollsters use the Likely Voter Cutoff Model (LVCM), a series of questions regarding past voting history, residential transience, intent to vote, etc. Since students, transients, low-income voters, immigrant new voters, etc. are much more likely to give "No" answers than established, wealthier, non-transient voters,

Republicans are more likely to exceed the cutoff than Democrats. A respondent who indicates "yes" to four out of seven questions might be down-weighted to 50% compared to one who answers "yes" to all seven.

The LVCM assigns a weight of zero to all respondents falling below the cutoff, thereby eliminating them from the sample. But these potential voters have more than a zero probability of voting. The number of "Yes" answers required to qualify as a likely voter is set based on how the pollster wants the sample to turn out. The more Republicans the pollster wants in the sample, the more "Yes" answers are required. This serves to eliminate many Democrats and skews the sample to the GOP.

All pre-election polls interview registered voters. Likely Voter (LV) polls are a subset of the full Registered Voter (RV) sample. LV polls exclude most "new" registered voters – first-timers and others who did not vote in the prior election.

Pollsters have devised various methods for isolating the responses of "likely voters" using Likely Voter Cutoff Models. This is not a problem in exit polls, in which voters are questioned as they leave the voting area, but the widespread use of absentee voting in many states creates new problems.

The media primes voters before the election with LV-only projections and then covers up the fraud with final exit polls that they always force to match the vote miscounts.

Democrats always do better in the full RV sample than in the LV sub-sample. LV polls exclude millions of registered voters who actually vote – and most of them are Democrats. The media/pollster drumbeat of a "horse race" is largely based on the LV polls. The focus on LV polls conditions the public to expect a recorded vote which in fact will surely understate the True Democratic share.

The pollsters discount the RV sample, fully expecting that their LV projections will be a close match to a fraudulent recorded vote – but they never mention the F-word. They know that votes are miscounted in every election. And so their final LV-based poll predictions are usually quite accurate. Pollsters are paid to predict the recorded vote – not the True Vote.

As Election Day approaches, the MSM gradually phases out RV polls for LV polls which lowball the projected Democratic vote share. And so the general public is prepared for the fraudulent recorded vote-counts that the MSM knows are coming.

Since 2000, LV projections have closely matched recorded vote shares while RV poll projections closely matched unadjusted and preliminary state and national exit polls. In each election, the final exit polls were forced to match the recorded vote.

In 2004 and 2008, the Final National Exit Poll required impossible returning Bush voter turnout in order to match the recorded vote. Since pre-election LV poll predictions also matched the recorded vote, what can we conclude?

The media cites low Democratic enthusiasm in the 2010 midterms, but turnout will exceed the LV sub-sample. Most pollsters don't provide RV samples in the month prior to the election. The media will gush on how close the final LV predictions came to the vote but ignore the real reason: systemic election fraud.

In 2004, there were 22 million voters who did not vote in 2000. Nearly 60% of newly registered voters were Democrats. In the 2006 midterms, a Democratic tsunami gave them control of both houses. In 2008, there were approximately 15 million new voters of whom 70% voted for Obama.

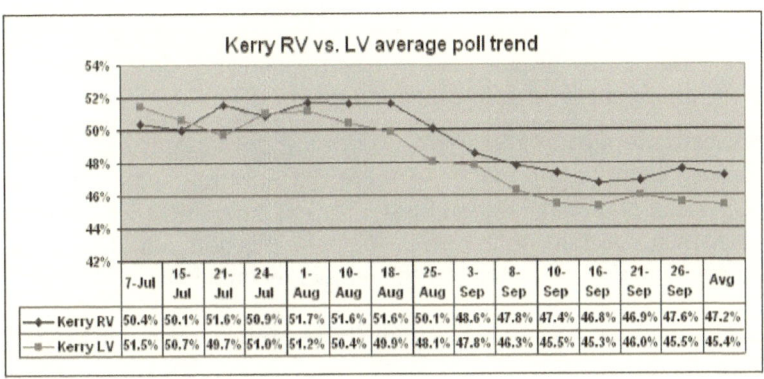

	7-Jul	15-Jul	21-Jul	24-Jul	1-Aug	10-Aug	18-Aug	25-Aug	3-Sep	8-Sep	10-Sep	16-Sep	21-Sep	26-Sep	Avg
Kerry RV	50.4%	50.1%	51.6%	50.9%	51.7%	51.6%	51.6%	50.1%	48.6%	47.8%	47.4%	46.8%	46.9%	47.6%	47.2%
Kerry LV	51.5%	50.7%	49.7%	51.0%	51.2%	50.4%	49.9%	48.1%	47.8%	46.3%	45.5%	45.3%	46.0%	45.5%	45.4%

Kerry RV vs. LV average poll trend

Projections based on final pre-election LV polls underestimated voter turnout but closely matched impossible final exit polls and fraudulent recorded vote counts. Projections based on final pre-election RV polls (after allocating undecided voters) closely match unadjusted exit polls and the True Vote.

Recorded vote share = LV projection
= RV projection + Fraud component

Recorded vote share = Final Exit Poll
= Unadjusted exit poll + Fraud component

Projections that ignore RV polls and focus solely on LV polls will inevitably underestimate the Democratic share, especially in heavy-turnout elections such as 2004 and 2008. In 2004, final pre-election projections were based on LV polls which understated voter turnout by 6%. Virtually all online political sites displayed LV polls (not RVs) and failed to allocate undecided voters.

Mainstream pollsters allocated 65-90% of undecided voters to Kerry. His projected national LV poll share was 1-2% lower than the projected RV share. In New York and California, pre-election poll projections were a virtual match to the recorded vote-count share. But they were 5-6% below Kerry's exit polls and True Vote shares.

The same LV/RV mismatch occurred in 2008. Obama had a 53% projection based on LV polls but had 57% based on RV national polls after allocating undecided voters.

In academic survey research, surveys are not designed to predict future events, but rather to analyse existing patterns. The American National Election Study, for example, includes both pre and post election interviews. In post election surveys, some respondents report voting for the winner, even when they did not.

The American National Election Study split its sample between face to face and telephone interviews for its 2000 pre-election survey. The response rate was 64.8% face- to-face and 57.2% for the telephone. The face-to-face surveys were generally more representative of the demographic characteristics of the general population. Telephone surveys produce response rates far lower than ANES.

Another approach is the online poll in which the "interaction" is conducted over the Internet. These are less expensive than traditional telephone surveys and larger samples are feasible. But they are not true random samples.

When samples differ from known characteristics of the population, they can be weighted to compensate for under or over representation of certain groups. There is still no way of knowing, however, whether respondents and non-respondents within these groups differ in their political attitudes and behaviour.

Uncounted Votes, Turnout and Final Exit Polls

In the final weeks prior to the 2004 and 2008 elections, national LV polls were displayed on political websites; many did not allocate undecided voters.

In Florida 2000, approximately 185,000 punch cards were under and over-punched. According to the Census, 43,000 more votes were cast than recorded. Where did the 142,000 extra votes come from? Bush won Florida by 537 votes.

In Florida 2004, according to the Census, approximately 238,000 more votes were recorded than cast. How many were uncounted? Bush won by 380,000 votes.

In Ohio 2004, according to the Census, 143,000 more votes were recorded than cast. Approximately 300,000 were uncounted. How many votes were switched? Bush won by 119,000 votes.

In 1988, 11 million votes were uncounted; in 2000, 6 million; in 2004, 4 million; in 2006, 3 million. Projections based on final pre-election LV polls closely matched fraudulent recorded vote shares. Projections based on the final pre-election RV polls closely matched the unadjusted exit polls.

Undecided voters typically break heavily for the challenger. In each of the last three elections, the Democrats were the challengers, but many pollsters did not allocate accordingly. Democratic voter turnout was underestimated by the pre-election LV polls (see 2004 Final Pre-election polls).

Uncounted votes have steadily declined as percent of total votes cast – from 10.4% in 1988 to 2.7% in 2004. When added to the recorded vote in order to derive total votes cast from 1988-2004, the average Democratic unadjusted exit poll share was within 1% of the adjusted vote. But the 2004 exit poll discrepancies were different in kind and scope from the prior elections; the discrepancies cannot be explained by uncounted votes alone.

Forecasters who predicted a Bush win in 2000 and 2004 were only "correct" because of rigged recorded vote counts. Gore won the recorded vote by 540,000; he won the True Vote by 3 million. Kerry lost the recorded vote by 3 million; he won the True Vote by 10 million. The pattern continued in 2008. Obama won the recorded vote by 9.5 million; he won the True Vote by nearly 23 million.

In 2004, Bush won the official recorded vote by 50.7-48.4%. Kerry had a slight 1% lead in the weighted pre-election state and national polls. After allocating the undecided voters, he was projected to win by 51.4-47.7%.

In the state exit polls, 76,000 voters were sampled. Kerry won the unadjusted aggregate by 51.1-47.5%.

For Bush to obtain his 3.0 million vote margin, he required 22% of returning Gore voters! The Final National Exit Poll was forced to match the recorded vote.

Typically 600 voters were surveyed in the state pre-election poll (4% margin of error). In 18 national pre-election polls, the samples ranged from 800 (3.5%) to 3500 (1.7%).

Based on historic evidence, the challenger is normally expected to win the majority (60-90%) of undecided voters, depending on incumbent job performance. Bush had a 48% approval rating on Election Day. Gallup allocated 90% of undecided voters to Kerry, pollsters Zogby and Harris allocated 75-80%.

The National Exit Poll indicated that Kerry won late undecided voters by a 12% margin over Bush. In the final national exit polls, Kerry had a 51.6% share with a 94.5% popular vote win probability.

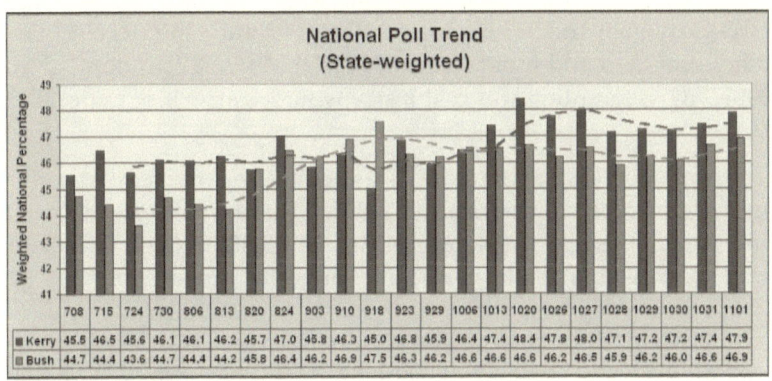

	708	715	724	730	806	813	820	824	903	910	918	923	929	1006	1013	1020	1026	1027	1028	1029	1030	1031	1101
■ Kerry	45.5	46.5	45.6	46.1	46.1	46.2	45.7	47.0	45.8	46.3	45.0	46.8	45.9	46.4	47.4	48.4	47.9	48.0	47.1	47.2	47.2	47.4	47.9
▣ Bush	44.7	44.4	43.6	44.7	44.4	44.2	45.8	46.4	46.2	46.9	47.5	46.3	46.2	46.6	46.6	46.6	46.2	46.5	45.9	46.2	46.0	46.6	46.9

Monte Carlo Simulation Methodology

Simulation is widely used in many diverse applications when an analytical solution is prohibitive.

The purpose of an electoral vote simulation is to calculate the overall probability of winning the electoral vote. The probability is the ratio of the number of winning election trials to the total number of trials.

The probability of winning the state popular vote is based on the 2-party projected vote share and an estimated margin of error. The projection determines the probability of winning a state which is input to the simulation.

The state win probability is determined by the poll shares (after allocating undecided voters) and the poll's margin of error. These are input to the Excel normal distribution function. The simulation generates an electoral vote win probability that is insensitive to minor changes in the state polls.

The expected (theoretical) electoral vote does not require a simulation. It is calculated by a simple summation formula: the product sum of the state win probabilities and corresponding electoral votes.

2004 Election Model

The final Election Model forecast had Kerry winning 51.8% of the two-party vote and 337 electoral votes. State and national elections were projected and input to the 5000 trial Monte Carlo simulation. The only assumption was that Kerry would win 75% of undecided voters.

The only forecast assumption was estimating the allocation of undecided voters. Historically, 70-80% of undecided voters break for the challenger. If the race is tied at 45-45, a 60-40% split of undecided voters results in a 51-49% projected vote share.

The model executed 5000 election trials in deriving the EV win probability. The average (mean) electoral vote approaches the theoretical EV as the number of trials increased, an illustration of the Law of Large Numbers (LLN). The mean (average) and median (central value) electoral vote is within 2% of the theoretical mean after just 500 trials.

The probability of capturing at least 270 electoral votes is just the number of winning trials divided by the total number of trials. Kerry had a 99.8% win probability based on the Monte Carlo Electoral Vote Simulation (he won 4995 of 5000 trials).

The model displayed a sensitivity (risk) analysis based on five undecided voter (UVA) scenario assumptions. The purpose was to view the effects of UVA on the expected electoral vote and win probability.

Electoral vote forecasting models which do not provide a risk factor sensitivity analysis are incomplete.

2004 Election Simulation Model

This model calculates 200 election trials using final state pre-election polls and post-election exit polls. Regardless of the method used for state projections, state win probabilities are sufficient to calculate the expected electoral vote. a simulation is only required to calculate the electoral vote win probability.

In the pre-election model, state and national polls are adjusted for the allocation of undecided voters. The post-election model is based on unadjusted and adjusted state exit polls. Monte Carlo simulation is used to project state and aggregate vote shares and calculate the popular and electoral vote win probabilities.

A random number (RND) between 0 and 1 is generated and compared to the probability of winning the state. For example, if Kerry had a 90% probability of winning Oregon and RND was less than 0.90, Kerry wins 7 electoral votes. If the RND is greater than 0.90, Bush is the winner. The procedure is repeated for all 50 states and DC. The winner of the trial has at least 270 EV.

The electoral vote win probability is directly correlated to the probability of winning the national popular vote. But electoral vote win probabilities in models developed by academics and bloggers are often incompatible with the projected national vote shares.

For example, assume a 53% projected national vote share. If the corresponding EV win probability is 88%, the model design/logic is incorrect; the vote share and win probability are incompatible. For a 53% share, the win probability is virtually 100%.

It is strong circumstantial evidence that the election was stolen. The model uses a random process of repeated experimental "trials" applied to a mathematical system model.

A major advantage of the Monte Carlo method is that the win probability is not sensitive to minor deviations in the state polls. A projected 51% vote share has less electoral "weight" than a 52% share, etc.

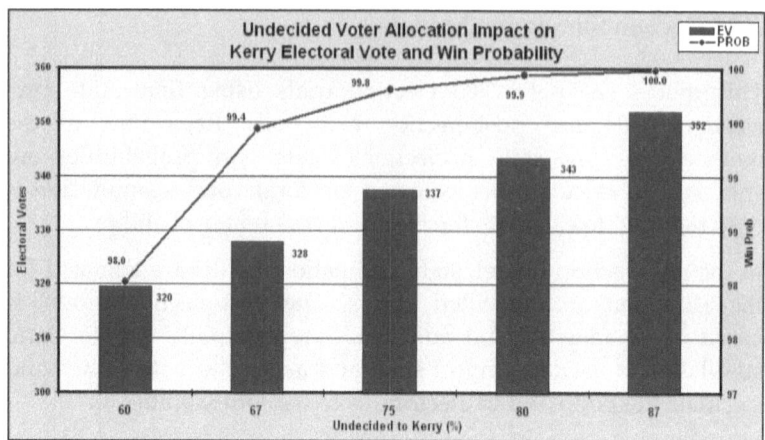

Snapshot Electoral Vote

Electoral vote projections from media pundits and Internet bloggers just total the electoral votes. It is a static picture, a snapshot of just one scenario. This can be misleading if the states are competitive (i.e. the poll margin is less than 3%).

Snapshot projections do not provide a robust expected electoral vote split and win probability. Unlike the Monte Carlo method, they fail to consider the two bedrocks of statistical analysis: The Law of Large Numbers and the Central Limit Theorem.

For example, consider a poll shift from 46-45 to 45-46. This would have a major impact in the electoral vote. But in a Monte Carlo simulation, the change would have just a minimal effect on the expected (average) electoral vote and win probability. The 46-45 poll split means that the race is too close to clearly project a winner; both candidates have a nearly equal win probability.

The large discrepancy between the exit polls and the vote count indicates that either a) the pre-election and unadjusted exit polls were faulty or b) the votes were miscounted, or c) a combination of both. Much other confirming evidence indicates that the votes were miscounted for Bush.

The True Vote always differs from the official recorded vote due to uncounted, switched and stuffed ballots. Were the pollsters who forecast a Bush win correct? Or were Zogby and Harris correct in projecting a Kerry win? None of the pollsters mentioned the election fraud factor – the most important variable of all.

2008 Election Model

In 2008, Obama won the recorded vote by 52.9-45.6%, matching the likely voter (LV) polls. Registered voter (RV) polls indicated that he would win 57%.

The model exactly matched Obama's 365 EV. His win probability was 100% since he won all 5000 election trials. His projected 53.1% share was a close match to the recorded 52.9%. But the model was wrong.

Pre-election likely voter (LV) polls understated Obama's vote. The registered voter (RV) polls projected Obama to win 57%. The pre-election polls were confirmed by the post-election True Vote Model (58%, 420 EV) and the unadjusted state exit polls that are never mentioned in the media.

But the real whopper is the fact that Obama won the unadjusted National Exit Poll by 61-37% (17,836 respondents).

Political pundits avoid the following critical factors:
- Votes cast compared to recorded (uncounted ballots)
- Underestimated turnout of newly registered voters
- Undecided voter allocation
- Voter mortality in estimating returning voter turnout
- Correlation of vote shares vs. approval ratings, Party-ID, etc.
- Feasible estimates of returning voters from the prior election
- Returning voters cannot exceed the number still living

CHAPTER 4

Exit Poll Magic

I can believe anything provided that it is quite incredible
- Oscar Wilde

The Oct. 2012 decision to eliminate exit polls in 19 states by the National Election Pool is a blow to Election Integrity. Unadjusted state exit poll data have been a major component in calculating exit poll discrepancies. Of course, we don't get to see the unadjusted exit poll numbers until months or years after the election.

The Director of Elections for ABC News, a member of the consortium that runs the exit poll, said the aim is to still deliver a quality product in the most important states, in the face of mounting survey costs, partially due to the continued rise in the number of cell phones which increases the cost of phone surveys.

He said that "the decision by the National Election Pool — a joint venture of the major television networks and The Associated Press — is sure to cause some pain to election watchers across the country". He's right about that. But how much is transparency in our elections worth?

These states will be excluded: Alaska, Arkansas, Delaware, District of Columbia, Georgia, Hawaii, Idaho, Kentucky, Louisiana, Nebraska, North Dakota, Oklahoma, Rhode Island, South Carolina, South Dakota, Tennessee, Texas, Utah, West Virginia and Wyoming.

Although not battleground states, they are still required to calculate the total weighted average National Vote Share. In fact, the unadjusted exit polls in these states showed that Obama did much better in the polls than the recorded vote. McCain led Obama by 3.4 million in the 19 states, but only by 1.1 million in the corresponding exit polls. Obama actually won the exit polls in Alaska, Nebraska and Georgia. He was exactly tied with McCain in South Dakota.

It will no longer be possible to compare the total weighted average of the state polls to the official recorded share. The full set of 1988-2008 unadjusted state-exit-polls statistical reference was required to show that the Democratic presidential candidates did nearly 8% better in unadjusted exit polls (52-42%) than the recorded vote (48-46%).

The discrepancies were due to a combination of uncounted votes and electronic vote switching. The uncounted vote rate declined, but electronic vote switching has taken up the slack.

The National Election Pool has never released unadjusted precinct exit poll data. Their transparent claim is the need for exit poll respondent confidentiality. It's a misleading canard; exit poll respondents do not reveal personal information.

In their 2004 report, the pollsters provided average Within Precinct Error (WPE) statistics for the 1988-2004 exit polls. That report provided more than enough historical information to hoist the NEP, the pollsters and the naysayers on their own petard.

Is the corporate media preparing for another 2004? The pollsters will provide the National Exit Poll, a subset of the state polls which includes just 20% of the respondents. But as it is standard operating procedure, the poll will be forced to match the recorded vote. It's a moot point, since we won't see the unadjusted, pristine poll numbers until long after the election, if then.

But we have the True Vote Model which can calculate the net defection of returning Obama voters that would be required to match the recorded vote. Maybe the TVM will provide some clues in lieu of the exit polls.

Exit polls are conducted in selected precincts that are chosen to represent the overall state population demographic. Voters are randomly selected as they leave the precinct polling booth and asked to complete a survey form indicating 1) who they just voted for, 2) how they voted in the previous election, 3) income range, 4) age group, 5) party-id (Democrat, Republican, Independent), 6) philosophy (liberal, moderate, conservative), and other questions.

The most important question: who did you vote for? Having this information, we calculate the discrepancy between the state exit poll and the recorded vote count.

Respondents are not asked to provide personal information. There is no privacy issue, but the media has never released actual raw precinct exit poll results. Exit polls are considered to be more accurate than pre-election and post-election telephone surveys for the basic reason that voters are interviewed immediately after they leave the polling booth.

But if exit polls are more accurate than pre-election polls, then why do the pundits claim that they vary from the official results and therefore are not that accurate after all. It's a contradiction. Does that make sense?

Like any other sample survey, exit polls have sampling, coverage, non-response, and measurement errors. But the errors are minimal compared to standard telephone surveys for two basic reasons. Voters are polled immediately after exiting the booth – and their responses are confidential.

Exit polls have several advantages over pre-election polls: Respondents are asked who they just voted for, as opposed to who they expect to vote for. They fill out a questionnaire in private, so that respondents may respond truthfully, greatly reducing their discomfort in disclosing their preferences on the phone.

Another advantage of exit polls is that questionnaires are from a much larger number of respondents than telephone surveys. Pre-election and post-election surveys typically interview between 500 and 1,500 respondents, with a 3-5% margin of error. National exit polls interviewed 12,000 to 18,000 with a 1.5% margin of error.

So why is it that since 1988, 226 of 274 exit polls deviated to the GOP? Why is it that the Democrats led the polls by 52-42% but won the recorded vote by just 48-46%?

And why is it that the margin of error was exceeded in 126 exit polls, of which an astounding 123 red-shifted to the Republican? Only 14 would be expected to exceed the margin of error.

Exit Poll Methodology

Sampling is a two-stage process. The first step is to choose a subset of precincts. The second is to determine a group of voters to interview in selected precincts.

National pollsters choose precincts by taking probability samples in each state before drawing a subsample from the state. Precincts are categorized by geographic region, usually between three to five regions in each state.

For each region, precincts are ordered by their percentage vote for one of the major political parties in a previous election. Precincts are sampled in proportion to the total votes cast in a prior election The samples in each state are combined. *A national sample of precincts is selected from them using a previous presidential race to determine the relative number of precincts chosen from each state.* A national exit poll includes 250-300 precincts.

Within each precinct, interviewers interview every 10th voter. The proportion of refusals varies by precinct, but typically it occurs in roughly a third of voters in the sample. *Could it be that more Democrats respond simply because there are more Democratic voters?*

Once this discrepancy has been corrected by weighting the exit polls to correspond with the actual vote, there has been no evidence that the vote estimates within groups are biased. *The Democrats are penalized because more of them voted than the Republicans?*

Many voters cast ballots in advance by mail or at designated locations. Citizens living overseas, deployed by the military, or away at school were permitted to mail an absentee ballot to the precinct of permanent residence. A growing number of states have permitted anyone registered to vote early, regardless of their rationale, in an effort to stimulate participation. *Republicans seek to limit the number of eligible voters.*

Some states permit voters to mail in early/ absentee ballots. Others require voters to submit early/absentee ballots at designated locations. By 2010, approximately 30% of ballots were cast early.

National exit pollsters account for early/absentee voting by conducting telephone surveys. By 2008, NEP was conducting telephone surveys in eighteen states, including Oregon, Washington, and Colorado, where early voting rates were so high to preclude exit polls. *Is it just a coincidence that Oregon, Washington and Colorado, the states with the highest percentage of early voting, had the smallest exit poll discrepancies?*

On Election Day, the results from the absentee/early voter telephone surveys are combined with the on-site exit polls. After the election, the exit polls and absentee/early voter telephone surveys are forced to the proportions of the actual vote totals that they comprised in their respective states.

A centralized computing system receives exit poll results, completion rates, and turnout information from interviewers and tabulates responses to each question across all precincts in a given jurisdiction. The results are weighted to account for various sampling considerations. The findings are then integrated with cumulative precinct tallies of turnout and vote returns into various projection models to estimate vote totals for each candidate.

Initially, respondents are weighted for their probability of selection within a given precinct. This probability is based on how many people voted overall in the precinct and the composition of voters who failed to respond. Interviewers provide turnout numbers based on their own counts or those of precinct election officials. *Later in the process, as the actual final turnout figures become more available, they replace any remaining interviewers' estimates, often altering the weight in the process.*

Interviewers track the sex, race, and age of voters who were missed or chose not to participate. The frequency distribution of non-responders is then compared to responders. If different, the data are adjusted to account for discrepancies. *Precincts within a state are adjusted to match their relative size in the state's active electorate. The exit poll results are then weighted to match the state's voting population.*

Exit poll results are forced to the official turnout and the vote share given to the respective candidates in each precinct. In other words, the pollsters believe that it is unlikely that election fraud exists. How do they account for the impossible 119%, 110% and 103% turnout of returning Bush voters in 1992, 2000 and 2004?

The American Association of Public Opinion Research (AAPOR) state: *"What is important to note is that at the close of Election Day, exit poll results are weighted to reflect the actual election outcomes. It is in this way that the final exit poll data can be used for its primary and most important purpose – to shed light on why the election turned out the way it did. That is, exit polls are just as important for the information they gather about the voters' demographics and attitudinal predispositions towards the candidates and the campaign issues as they are for making the projections reported by news organizations on Election Night".*

The purpose of the final exit poll is to get accurate demographic data by matching to the actual vote count? Is this the way to conduct statistical research, by adjusting the results to fit the recorded vote? What if the vote count is corrupted? They never even ask the question. AAPOR refers to challenges facing exit pollsters, but they ignore the challenge of calculating the impact of election fraud on the recorded vote. The charade continues unabated.

If the vote counts were accurate, the demographics would be correct. Since the recorded vote counts are bogus, so are the demographics. Assuming the vote count is pristine immediately invalidates the demographic statistics. AAPOR would surely want to see the pristine, unadjusted exit poll data. One would assume that this august group would want to see it. But in their world, corruption is non-existent. They believe that the Recorded Vote is identical to the True Vote.

AAPOR claims that: *"An exit poll sample is not representative of the entire electorate until the survey is completed at the end of the day. Different types of voters turn out at different times of the day".*

But there is no mention that Kerry led the exit polls by a steady 51-48% from 4:00 pm (8349 sampled) to 7:30 pm (11,027) and 12:22 am (13,047) to the final 13,660. Or that uncounted votes are 70-80% Democratic and contribute significantly to the exit poll discrepancies.

AAPOR repeats the Reluctant Bush Responder (rBr) myth used by exit pollsters Edison-Mitofsky: *"In recent national and state elections, Republicans have declined to fill out an exit poll questionnaire at a higher rate than Democratic voters, producing a slight Democratic skew".*

But the 2004 Final Exit Poll indicated that Bush 2000 voters comprised 43% of the 2004 electorate (which was mathematically impossible) as opposed to 37% of Gore voters. According to the *2004 Exit Poll Evaluation Report* report, the highest exit poll refusal rates were in Democratic states.

"Research has shown that the characteristics of early/absentee voters can be quite different from Election Day precinct voters, and this difference is capable of skewing exit poll findings".

Yes, like the characteristic of vote rigging.

"Exit poll results can be skewed by non-response error when sampled respondents fail to complete the questionnaire. This omission could bias results if certain groups respond at different rates".

Who is not responding? The pundits want us to believe it's the Democrats. But the data shows otherwise. It's the same old canard. Repeat it often enough and people will believe it.

"Republican voters are less likely than their Democratic counterparts to complete exit polls".

But they cannot explain the ZERO probabilities of the 274 state exit poll discrepancies from 1988-2008.

"In 1992, the preliminary exit poll results showed an apparent partisan skew. They overstated Bill Clinton's share of the vote by 2.5 points in the 1992 presidential race. Exit pollster Warren Mitofsky claimed the discrepancy was due to partisan differences in the willingness of voters to complete the exit poll. It was not due to a poor selection of precincts or differential response rates by age, race, or gender. Mitofsky speculated that Democratic voters were more excited about voting for Clinton than Republican voters for Bush".

The 1992 reluctant Bush responder theory was a prologue of 2004. Mitofsky was never asked about the 119% turnout of living 1988

Bush voters that was required to force the National Exit Poll to match the match the recorded vote. Perhaps it was because the pundits did not bother to do the simple math.

"In 2000, at 7:50 pm statistical models predicted Al Gore the winner in Florida. Pundits claimed that since only 4 percent of the actual vote had been counted and numerous precincts in the Florida panhandle were open until 8 p.m., the polls were not accurate".

But the fact that just 4% of the total votes were counted is immaterial. The only number that counts is the number of voters who were exit polled. Sampling was done throughout the day.

"Less than ten minutes later, the networks and the AP announced Gore the winner in Florida. But according to VNS, vote-count data from Duval County was entered incorrectly, giving Gore more votes than he actually did. The networks announced they were moving the state back to the undecided category".

Months later we learned that in Duval and other counties, there were 185,000 spoiled ballots, of which 113,000s were double and triple punched. In Volusia County 16,022 votes were deducted from Gore. Dan Rather called it a "glitch". Gore won the exit poll by 50-45%.

"With 97 percent of the precincts reporting, Bush had a 50,000 vote lead. At 2:15 a.m., Fox News called Florida and the presidency for Bush. Within five minutes, NBC, CNN, CBS, and ABC followed. But VNS and the AP chose not to call the race in Florida a second time, wary of the volatility in the data with the contest that close. During the next couple hours, new errors were discovered. VNS had underestimated the number of votes remaining to be counted. Two counties – Volusia and Brevard – had "mistakenly" entered their vote totals in favor of Bush. Once these "mistakes" were corrected, the race narrowed. Bush's lead was inside the margin of error".

We know about Volusia and Brevard, but what about the other counties? How many votes did Gore lose to the Palm Beach County butterfly ballot? There were nearly 200,000 spoiled ballots in Florida – and 75% were for Gore. But this fact is never mentioned in the media. Even Al Gore won't talk about it today.

"Around 4 a.m., the networks began retracting their calls for Bush, announcing that a recount would be necessary. But it was too late. Morning headlines announced that Bush was elected. But the exit polls were no longer a factor, as they were replaced by actual vote counts – incorrect as they were in some cases – over the course of the evening".

Forcing the exit polls to match the recorded vote is a standard operating procedure that the media has never discussed.

"In the 2002 midterms, strangely, the new VNS computer system failed to properly integrate and analyse information imported from precincts around the country. The AP was running a backup operation. VNS was unable to supply exit poll data. The media wanted explanations for the election anomalies".

Was it really a computer system failure? Pre-election polls showed the Democrats winning. What did the exit polls show? WE will never know. At least three senate elections were stolen.

"Within a month, the National Election Pool (NEP) was formed to oversee the administration of a single, joint exit poll. The NEP hired Edison Research, which had served as the backup system for CNN in the 2002 election, and Mitofsky International, to conduct the exit polls. Edison/Mitofsky would make projections, but each network would be responsible for the calls they made on the air. In 2004, Edison/Mitofsky did not make any incorrect projections on Election Day".

But how could they? The projections were forced to conform to the recorded vote.

"The pollsters claimed that preliminary data overstated the difference in the George W. Bush-John Kerry vote on election night by 5.5 percentage points, predicting a 51- to 48-percent advantage for Kerry rather than a 50.5- to 48-percent win for Bush".

In fact, the exit polls showed that Kerry led from start to finish. Exit pollster Mitofsky claimed (as he did in 1992) that Bush voters were reluctant to speak to the exit pollsters, but his own 2004 Evaluation Report showed just the opposite: the highest response rates were in partisan Bush precincts. Unfortunately, the media pundits did not read the 77-page report so they never questioned it. Or if they did read it, they chose to ignore it.

In Jan. 2005, the exit pollster's precinct data indicated that Kerry had 52.0% and 337 electoral votes. Kerry had 51.0% in the unadjusted state exit poll aggregate (76,192 respondents) and 51.7% in the National Exit Poll (13,660). But it was not enough to overcome the massive fraud which gave Bush a 3.0 million vote "mandate". The post-election True Vote Model indicated he had 53.5%– a 10 million vote landslide.

Mitofsky claimed that the average 6.5% "within precinct error" was due to a systematic bias in the selection of voters, but that the precincts were representative of the states. He repeated the 1992 canard that Bush voters were more likely to refuse to participate in the exit polls than Kerry voters. He hypothesized that the discrepancy was due to interviewers under age thirty-five, perhaps because they were correctly perceived to have been more likely to vote for Kerry. But he ignored his own data, which showed that exit poll response was higher in partisan Bush precincts – and in Bush states.

"The pollsters claimed that voting patterns within groups were accurate once they were weighted to the official results. They found no evidence that the distribution of vote choices within various demographic groups was biased, despite the vote choice of exit poll respondents overall overstating Democratic support".

In other words, the poll was accurate after it was weighted to the official results?

"In the aftermath of the 2004 election, Edison/Mitofsky announced they would make several changes to address these issues. They committed to hiring interviewers from a broader age range. And they would not release any results from the exit polls prior to 6 p.m. eastern time".

In 2008 Obama won the recorded vote by 52.9-45.6%. But he won the National Exit Poll by 61-37% and won the state exit poll aggregate by 58-40.5%. So how do the pollsters explain the massive 2008 exit poll discrepancy? They don't. There is just one explanation but the pollsters and the media won't go there.

CHAPTER 5

Red Shift

Facts do not cease to exist because they are ignored
- Aldous Huxley

The analysis of state and national exit poll discrepancies in the 1988-2008 presidential elections just got easier. In 2011, I entered unadjusted exit polls data from the Roper Center for Public Opinion into an online spreadsheet to enable a comparative analysis of state exit polls and recorded votes. The link is on *richardcharnin.com* and on my blog.

Now we know what the respondents actually said as to how they voted – fundamental information that was not previously available. It is not the raw precinct level data that analysts would love to see and which the corporate media (the National Election Pool) will not release. Nevertheless, the unadjusted data is the mother-lode for serious exit poll analysis. The pattern is clear: the Democrats always do better in the polls than in the recorded count. There is no evidence that this one-sided result is due to anything other than vote miscounts.

The one-sided results of 375,000 state exit poll respondents over the last six presidential elections leads to only one conclusion: the massive exit poll discrepancies cannot be due to faulty polling and is overwhelming evidence that systemic election fraud has favoured the Republicans in every election since 1988. Fraud certainly cost the Democrats at least two elections (2000, 2004) and likely a third (1988). And in the three elections they won, their margin was reduced significantly by election fraud.

Unadjusted exit poll data reflect actual samples. Vote shares have closely matched the corresponding True Vote Model, which calculates feasible estimates of returning and new voters. But exit poll demographics displayed in the mainstream media are always forced to match the recorded vote by "adjusting" the category crosstab weightings and/or vote shares. Final adjusted exit polls do not reflect actual voter response, but merely parrot the recorded (fraudulent) vote. The fraud factor is assumed to be zero in the final published polls.

To force State and National Exit Polls to match the recorded vote, all demographic category weights and/or vote shares must be adjusted.

Presidential election exit poll data is archived on the Roper University of Connecticut website. It consists of 50 state files (and Washington DC) in PDF format. In order to utilize the 1988-2008 presidential data for meaningful analysis, I formatted and consolidated the files into a single spreadsheet containing individual election worksheets. Other sheets contained supplementary graphs and tables.

Vanishing Probabilities

In the 1988-2008 presidential elections, 274 states were exit polled. An analysis of the unadjusted exit poll discrepancies from the recorded vote shows that Republicans did better in the recorded vote than the exit poll in 226 (82.4%) of the 274 elections. The probability of this one- sided red-shift is virtually ZERO: 1 in 2.7 million trillion trillion. If the elections were fraud-free, an approximate 50% shift would normally be expected.

The Republicans won the recorded vote in 55 states in which the Democrats won the exit poll. Conversely, the Republicans lost the recorded vote in just two states (Iowa and Minnesota in 2000) in which they won the exit poll. If the elections were fair, the number of vote flips would be nearly equal. The probability of this disparity is virtually ZERO.

The probability is 1 in 88 trillion that 55 of 57 exit polls would flip from the Democrats to the Republicans in the recorded vote

The exit poll **margin of error** (described below) was exceeded in 126 (46%) of the 274 polls. The statistical expectation is that the margin of error (MoE) would be exceeded in 14 (5%). The probability is ZERO.

The probability that the exit poll margin of error would be exceeded in any given state is 5% or 1 in 20. Given a 95% level of confidence, approximately 14 of 274 exit polls would be expected to fall outside the margin of error (7 for the Republican and 7 for the Democrat). But it was exceeded in 126 elections, all but three in favor of the Republicans.

The probability is ZERO that it was due to chance. Well, almost. *It's 1 in 1.8 billion trillion trillion trillion trillion trillion trillion trillion trillion.*

The one-sided red-shift to the Republican implies that the exit polls were systemically incorrect or that the votes were miscounted. It could not have been due to chance. Exit polls are known to be quite accurate – outside the USA.

Were the discrepancies due to Republican voter reluctance to be polled in each of the 274 state elections? Were they due to Democratic voters misstating how they voted to the exit pollsters? Or were they due to the millions of mostly Democratic votes that were uncounted and miscounted in favor of the Republican? That is quite likely.

It has long been established that state and national exit polls are always forced to match the recorded vote, often with impossible returning voter weights. The unadjusted data shows just how the exit pollsters had to adjust the actual responses to force the match.

Furthermore, and most important, the data confirms True Vote Model calculations in each election. The pattern of massive discrepancies confirms that the adjusted Final National Election Poll is fiction and debunks the corresponding myth that elections are fair and that the votes are counted accurately. The 1988-2008 unadjusted state and national exit polls (and the True Vote Model) indicate the Democrats won by an 8% higher margin than recorded.

Media polling pollsters, pundits and academics need to do a comparable scientific analysis of historical exit polls and create their own True Vote models. So-called independent journalists need to discuss the devil in the details of systemic election fraud. They can start by trying to debunk the analysis presented here.

Election	1988	1992	1996	2000	2004	2008	Average
Recorded Vote							
Democrat	45.7	43.0	49.3	48.4	48.3	52.9	47.9
Republican	53.4	37.4	40.7	47.9	50.7	45.6	46.0
Unadjusted Aggregate State Exit Polls							
Democrat	50.3	47.6	52.6	50.8	51.1	58.0	51.7
Republican	48.7	31.7	37.1	44.4	47.5	40.3	41.6
Unadjusted National Exit Poll							
Democrat	49.8	46.3	52.0	48.5	51.7	61.0	51.6
Republican	49.2	33.5	37.1	46.3	47.0	37.2	41.7

1988

Dukakis won the unadjusted National Exit Poll (11,645 respondents) by 49.6-48.4% (11,645 respondents). He won the exit polls in the battleground states by 51.6-47.3%. But Bush won by 7 million recorded votes. There were 11 million mostly Democratic uncounted votes.

As indicated above, 24 state exit polls are listed for 1988 on the Roper Center site. These states accounted for 68.7 (75%) of 91.6 million national recorded votes. Dukakis led the 24-poll aggregate by a 51.6-47.3%, but Bush won the corresponding recorded vote by 52.3-46.8%, a 9.8% margin discrepancy. The exit poll margin of error was exceeded in 11 of the 24 states – all in favor of Bush (see the summary statistics at the bottom).

Dukakis also won the unadjusted National Exit Poll by 49.8-49.2% – but Bush won by 7 million votes, 53.4-45.6%. According to the U.S. Census, 102.2 million votes were cast and 91.6 million recorded, therefore a minimum of 10.6 million ballots were uncounted.

Dukakis had approximately 8 million (75%) of the uncounted votes. Of course, voters whose ballots were uncounted were interviewed by the exit pollsters. That may be one of the reasons why Dukakis won the state and national exit polls and lost the recorded vote.

1992

Clinton won the unadjusted state exit polls (54,000 respondents) by 18 million votes (47.6-31.7%). He won the unadjusted National Exit Poll (15,000 respondents) by 46.3-33.4%. He had 51% in the True Vote Model (TVM). But his recorded margin was just 5.6 million (43.0-37.5%). The Final National Exit Poll (NEP) was forced to match the recorded vote. It implied a 119% turnout of living 1988 Bush voters. There were 10 million uncounted votes. The landslide was denied.

1996

Clinton won the unadjusted exit polls (70,000 respondents) by 16 million votes (52.6-37.1%). His recorded margin was 8 million (49.2-40.8%). He had 53.6% in the TVM. The Final National Exit Poll (NEP) was forced to match the recorded vote. There were 10 million uncounted votes. The landslide was denied.

2000

Unadjusted State Exit Polls indicate that Al Gore won a mini-landslide in 2000. First there was the 2000 Judicial Coup and then the long-running media con that Bush really did win. Let's take another look.

Gore won the unadjusted state exit polls (58,000 respondents) by 6 million votes (50.8-44.4%). He had 51.5% in the TVM. He won the recorded vote by just 540,000. There were 6 million uncounted votes. The election was stolen. He won the unadjusted state exit polls (58,000 respondents) by 50.8-44.4%, a 6 million vote margin compared to the 540,000 recorded. There were nearly 6 million uncounted votes. The vast majority were for Gore.

The True Vote Model closely matched Gore's exit poll share. He had a 50.0% True share assuming he had 75% of 8 million returning 1996 voters whose ballots were uncounted and 75% of 6 million uncounted votes in 2000.

Bush won Florida by 537 votes. The recount was aborted in a 5-4 Supreme Court decision. But it was not even close. Gore won by at least 100,000 votes. There were 185,000 uncounted ballots: 110,000 were over-punched and 75,000 under-punched. And thousands of butterfly ballots were mistakenly marked for Buchanan in heavily Democratic Palm Beach County.

Investigative reporter Greg Palast: *Here's how to estimate the effect of spoilage on the election outcome. For fun, let's take Florida 2000. We know from comparison of census tracts to precincts that 54% of the 179,855 ballots spoiled were cast by African-American voters, that is, 97,000 of the total. Every poll put the black vote in Florida for Al Gore at over 90%.*

Reasonably assuming "spoiled" ballots matched the typical racial preferences, Gore lost more than 87,000 votes in the spoilage pile. Less than 10% of the African-American population voted for Mr. Bush, i.e. Bush lost no more than 10,000 votes to spoilage. The net effect: Gore had a plurality of at least 77,000 within the uncounted ballots cast by black citizens.

Palast's estimate of spoiled ballots did not include thousands of absentee, provisional or stuffed ballots. Or the unknown number of Gore votes that were dropped or switched to Bush in cyberspace.

Gore won the unadjusted Florida exit poll (1816 respondents) by 53.4-43.6%. The margin of error was 3.0% (including a 30% cluster effect). Based on these numbers, there is a 97.5% probability that Gore won Florida by a minimum of 200,000 votes. Florida was not unique. The 9.8% discrepancy was exceeded in 10 other states.

2004

Bush won the recorded vote by 50.7-48.3%. The average 6.5% (WPE) discrepancy indicated that Kerry won by 51.5-47.2%. The exit pollsters hypothesized that the discrepancy was due to 56 Kerry responders for every 50 Bush responders. But it was just a guess. In fact, precinct votes by partisanship groupings showed that Bush voters were slightly more responsive.

The *composite* state exit polls were downloaded from the CNN election site by Jonathan Simon. The polls were already in the process of being adjusted to incoming vote counts and weighted to include pre-election polls (the *"composite"*). Adjustments made around 1:00 am forced a perfect match to the recorded votes.

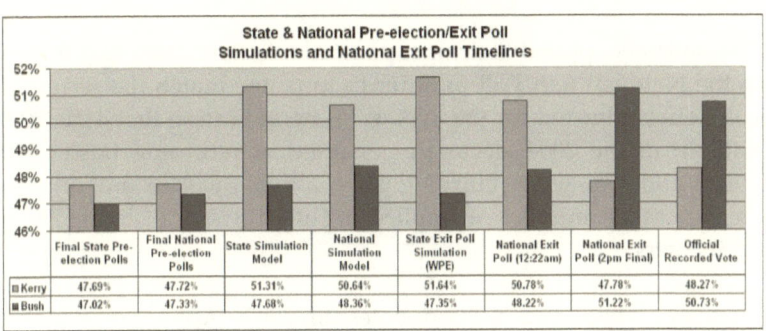

	Final State Pre-election Polls	Final National Pre-election Polls	State Simulation Model	National Simulation Model	State Exit Poll Simulation (WPE)	National Exit Poll (12:22am)	National Exit Poll (2pm Final)	Official Recorded Vote
□ Kerry	47.69%	47.72%	51.31%	50.64%	51.64%	50.78%	47.78%	48.27%
■ Bush	47.02%	47.33%	47.68%	48.36%	47.35%	48.22%	51.22%	50.73%

State and national exit poll discrepancies are calculated in two ways. The WPD is the difference between the **average exit poll precinct** margin and the **average precinct recorded vote** margin. The unadjusted exit poll discrepancy is the difference between the **actual total exit poll respondent** margin and the **total recorded vote** margin. The exit pollsters provided the average Within Precinct Error (WPE) for each state. But that implies that the exit poll was in error, so let's refer to it as Within Precinct Discrepancy (WPD).

A positive WPD indicates that the vote shift favored the GOP; a negative WPD favored the Democrat. In 2004, Kerry won the state exit polls by 52-47% but lost the recorded vote by 50.7-48.3%, a WPD of 7.4%.

In the 2004 NY election Kerry won the NY recorded vote by 58.4-40.1%, an 18.3% margin. The exit pollsters indicated a 12.2% WPD implying that Kerry had a 30.5% (64.5-34.0%) exit poll margin.

In the unadjusted NY exit poll (1452 respondents), Kerry had 901 (62.05%), Bush 525 (36.15%), Other 26 (1.80%). Kerry had a 25.9% unadjusted exit poll margin over Bush. The discrepancy was 7.6% (25.9-18.3). The margin of error includes a 30% cluster factor.

Kerry won the unadjusted state exit poll aggregate (76,000 respondents) by 51.1-47.5%. He won the unadjusted National Exit Poll (13,660 respondents) by 51.7-47.0%, a 6 million vote margin.
Kerry had 53.6%, a 10 million vote margin, in the True Vote Model - but lost by 3.0 million recorded votes. There were 4 million uncounted votes. The election was stolen.

The pollsters applied their unsupported reluctant Bush hypothesis to the National Exit Poll in order to force the match the recorded vote. They adjusted for the 6.5% WPE by indicating that 43% (52.6 million) of the 2004 electorate consisted of returning Bush 2000 voters and 37% were returning Gore voters. But 52.6 million was an impossible number; it implied a 110% turnout of living Bush 2000 voters.

Bush only had 50.5 million votes in 2000. Approximately 2.5 million died prior to the 2004 election and one million did not return to vote. Therefore, no more than 47 million Bush 2000 voters (38.4% of the 122.3 million) could have returned. **There had to be 5.6 million phantom Bush voters.**

Since the National poll was forced to match the recorded vote with an impossible number of returning Bush voters, the recorded vote must have been impossible. Simple mathematics proved election fraud.

In fact, Kerry led the unadjusted state exit poll aggregate (76,000 respondents) by 51.1-47.6%. He led the unadjusted National Exit Poll (13,660 respondents) by 51.7-47.0%. The True Vote Model (TVM) indicated that Kerry had 53.6%.

Why the difference between the TVM and the unadjusted state and national exit polls? The exit pollsters apparently designed their 2004 sample based on the 2000 recorded vote which indicated that Gore won by just 540,000 votes (48.4-47.9%). On the other hand, the TVM used a feasible estimate of returning voters from the prior election. Gore won the unadjusted state exit polls by 50.8-44.5% and the unadjusted National by 48.5-46.3%.

The distribution of the exit poll discrepancies in Democratic, GOP and Battleground states indicates that the GOP strategy was:

1) Pad Bush's popular vote "mandate" by cutting Democratic margins in heavily populated BLUE states:
NY, CA, CT, NJ, MD, MA and MI

2) Steal the electoral votes in Battleground states:
FL, OH, NM, CO, NV, MO and IA

3) Pad the vote in states with large minority voting blocs:
TX, MS, AL, TN, SC. Ignore ND, SD, OK, MT and KY

It should be obvious by now that final weighting adjustments made to the exit polls are made to match the recorded vote. In 2004, in addition to the impossible return voter mix, the 12:22 am National Exit Poll vote shares had to be adjusted in the Final NEP. The pollsters needed a 110% turnout of living 2000 Bush voters.

All exit poll demographic categories had to be adjusted to match the vote count. The following examples illustrate how the exit pollsters rigged the Final 2004 National Exit Poll demographic crosstabs to force a match the recorded vote.

Bush Approval

The unadjusted state exit poll weighted aggregate (76,000 respondents) indicates that 50.3% of respondents approved of Bush's performance. Kerry won the aggregate by 51.1-47.5%. He also won the unadjusted National Exit Poll, a 13,660 subsample, by 51.7-47.0%.

But in the adjusted Final National Exit Poll, Bush approval was increased to 53% to force a match to the recorded vote. Eleven (11) final national pre-election polls gave Bush a 48% approval rating.

Party-ID

The polls indicated a 38.8 D- 35.1 R- 26.1% I Party-ID split. But the Final National Exit Poll changed it to 37-37-26%. What was the rationale? In 2000, Democrats led by 39-35%.

In 2004, the vast majority of new voters were registered Democrats. The 37-37 split was not plausible; it was an artificial fudge to force a match to the recorded vote.

Ohio

Bush won the recorded vote by 50.8-48.7% (119,000 vote margin). Kerry won the exit poll by 54.1-45.7%, a 10.6% margin discrepancy. Which is correct, the poll or the recorded vote? How could there be such a wide disparity? In the exit poll, 2020 voters were sampled in approximately 40 precincts, of whom 1092 said they voted for Kerry (54.1%) and 924 for Bush (45.7%).

Given the exit poll data, we can calculate the probability of a) Kerry winning the election and b) of Bush getting his recorded vote share. The exit poll margin of error was 2.8%. Therefore, there is a 95.4% probability that the Kerry's True Vote was within 2.8% of his 54.1% exit poll share. The probability is 97.5% that Kerry had at least 51.3%. The normal distribution returned a 99.8% probability that Kerry won Ohio.

2008

Obama won the unadjusted state exit poll aggregate (83,000 respondents) by 58.0-40.3%, a 23 million vote margin - a near-exact match to the TVM. He won the unadjusted National Exit Poll (17,836 respondents) by a whopping 61-37%. Officially, he had 52.9% and won by 9.5 million votes. The landslide was denied.

As usual, the NEP was forced to match the recorded vote by indicating that returning Bush and Kerry voters comprised 46% and 37%, respectively, of the electorate. The pollsters implied that there were 12 million more returning Bush than Kerry voters. But Kerry won the unadjusted National Exit Poll by 6 million votes and the True Vote Model by 10 million.

The exit poll/vote margin discrepancy trend accelerated, exceeding 10% in 28 states.

It is instructive to see how the unadjusted 2008 exit polls compare to the recorded vote and the True Vote Model (TVM). The basic results are not surprising: Obama did better in the aggregate state exit polls (58.1%) than the vote count (52.9%). But the Democrats always do better in the polls. What is surprising is that he did 5.2% better – exactly matching the TVM. By way of comparison, Kerry did 3.7% better in the unadjusted exit polls (52%) than in the recorded vote (48.3%). He had 53.6% in the TVM.

In the National Exit Poll (NEP), 4178 of 17836 responders were asked how they voted in 2004. Of this subsample, 1815 (43.4%) said Kerry. 1614 (38.6%) Bush, 188 (4.5%) third-party and 561 (13.4%) did not vote.

Applying Final 2008 NEP vote shares to the returning voter mix, Obama had a 58.0% share – exactly matching his 58.0% share of the aggregate unadjusted state exit polls and the TVM share. The returning voter mix implied that Kerry won by 50.2-44.6%.

The pollsters needed an impossible 46/37% Bush/Kerry mix and implied that Bush won by 52.6-42.3%. His (bogus) recorded margin was 50.7-48.3%. Kerry won the True Vote with 53.6% (Table 6). In the Final 2008 NEP, pollsters effectively switched 269 of 1815 Kerry responders to Bush in order to force a match to the recorded vote – a 15% flip.

To summarize, the unadjusted 2008 NEP exactly matched the weighted aggregate share of the unadjusted state exit polls, based on how the exit poll responders said they voted in 2004 and 2008. It also matched the TVM which used 2004 votes cast, voter mortality, an estimate of living 2004 voter turnout in 2008 and 2008 NEP vote shares.

Obama had 58% in each calculation – a triple confirmation that he won a 23 million vote landslide, far exceeding his 9.5 million recorded vote margin.

But that's not all. The National Exit Poll of 17,836 respondents is a subset of the 82,000 sampled in the state exit polls. Obama won the unadjusted National Exit Poll by 61-37%, a landslide of historic proportions. However, the state exit polls have a smaller margin of error and are probably a better estimate of the True Vote.

The True Vote Model (TVM) is based on Census votes cast, mortality, prior election voter turnout and National Exit Poll vote shares. The TVM closely matched the exit polls in each election. It was within 0.1% of Obama's 58.0% unadjusted exit poll share.

Margin of Error Sensitivity Analysis

Sensitivity analysis is an important tool for viewing the effects of alternative assumptions in a mathematical model.

In pre-election polls, the margin of error (MoE) is based on the number of respondents. In exit polls, however, a *"cluster factor"* is added to the MoE. Therefore, the number of states in which the MoE was exceeded in 1988-2008 (and corresponding probabilities) is a function of the *cluster effect*.

In the six elections, the MoE was exceeded in 126 of 274 exit polls assuming a 30% cluster factor, the one most commonly used by political scientists and statisticians. The effect of a range of cluster factor assumptions on the number of state presidential exit polls in which the margin of error was exceeded is displayed in the *1988-2008 Unadjusted Exit Poll Database* (the link is on my website *richardcharnin.com*). The probability is zero that the margin of error would be exceeded in 126 state exit polls.

Were the discrepancies due to inferior polling by the most experienced media exit pollsters in the world or mathematical confirmation of systemic election fraud?

Pollsters and academics are welcome to peer-review the probability calculations which are based on classic mathematical functions applied to public data.

These states flipped from the Democrats in the exit poll to the GOP in the recorded vote.

1988 CA IL MD MI NM PA VT
Dukakis had a 51-47% edge in 24 battleground state polls and won the National Exit Poll by 50-49%. He lost by 7 million votes

1992 AK AL AZ FL IN MS NC OK TX VA
Clinton had an 18 million margin in the state exit polls. He won
the recorded vote by just 6 million.

1996 AK AL CO GA ID IN MS MT NC ND SC SD VA
Clinton had a 16 million margin in the polls and won by 8 million.

2000 AL AR AZ CO FL GA MO NC NV TN TX VA
Gore needed just one state to win the election. He won the exit
polls by 4-6 million, but the recorded vote by just 540,000.

2004 CO FL IA MO NM NV OH VA
Kerry won the national exit poll by 5-6 million with 51.7%. The
True Vote Model indicated he had 53.6% and won by 10 million.

2008 AL AK AZ GA MO MT NE
Obama had 58% in the state exit polls (a 23 million margin),
exactly matching the True Vote Model. He had 61% in the
unadjusted National Exit Poll.

CHAPTER 6

True Vote Model

When you have eliminated the impossible, whatever remains, however improbable, is the truth - Sir Arthur Conan Doyle

The corporate-funded exit pollsters match the recorded vote in every election. But as we have seen, the recorded vote never reflects the true intent of the voters. This is self-evident since the number of votes cast is never equal to the number recorded; therefore the True Vote shares cannot equal the recorded shares.

In the eleven elections since 1968, there were approximately 80 million net uncounted votes, declining from 10.6 million (10%) in 1988 to 5.4 million (5%) in 2000 to 3.4 million in 2004 (3%). Since the majority of uncounted voters are Democratic, they lose millions of votes in every election. Therefore we need to distinguish between the True Vote and the official, recorded vote provided by the media.

In the 1968-2008 presidential elections, the Republicans led the average recorded margin by 49-45%. The Democrats led the True Vote by 49-45%, an 8% margin discrepancy.

The National True Vote Model (TVM) is based on current and previous election votes cast (Census), voter mortality and returning voter turnout. National Exit Poll (NEP) vote shares were applied to new and returning voters. In the State True Vote Model, vote shares are derived from the national shares according to the state/national vote share ratio.

In order to disguise the exit poll discrepancies, implausible and/or impossible adjustments were required to force national and state exit polls to match the recorded vote. The most obvious adjustments were to the implied number of returning voters from the previous election, and are clearly indicated by the percentages of returning voters in the current election (the "mix").

The True Vote Model has closely matched the unadjusted state and national exit polls in every presidential election since 1988.

The unadjusted state exit poll is usually close to the corresponding True Vote. The aggregate unadjusted shares are a close match to the unadjusted National Exit Poll which closely approximates the National True Vote.

The Recursive True Vote Model (1968-2008)

The Recursive True Vote Model calculates the National True Vote for all elections since 1968. Data input consists of recorded and total votes cast. Returning voters from the prior election are estimated based on voter mortality and voter turnout. For the 1988-2008 elections, the final National Exit Poll shares are applied. For 1968-1988, the vote shares are calculated to match the recorded vote.

Starting with the 1968 election, the model sequentially derives a feasible returning vote mix from the prior election. True vote shares cast in the previous election are reduced by voter mortality and turnout in the current election and new voters are added to the mix. The process is recursive: the current election is a function of the prior.

Except for the 2004 election, the model uses Final National Exit Poll vote shares. In 2004 the Final NEP vote shares were radically adjusted to match the official tally. Therefore, preliminary 12:22am NEP vote shares were used to calculate the True Vote.

The model indicates that the 2000 and 2004 elections were definitely stolen and the 1968 and 1988 elections were likely stolen as well. In order for the national exit polls to match the official votes, there had to be a 94% average turnout of returning Democrats and 106% of Republicans. The average Republican turnout was an impossible 114% when Nixon and Bush were the incumbents; it was 98% in the other elections. The average True Vote discrepancy was 10.3% when Nixon and Bush were incumbents; it was 3.6% otherwise.

In 2008, Obama had a 58% True Vote share and 53% recorded. The True Vote was confirmed by at least 4 independent statistical measures: 1) Unadjusted National Exit Poll, 2) Unadjusted state exit polls, 3) True Vote Model and 4) 10 million late (paper ballot) votes. In the state polls, 82,000 were sampled. The average state exit poll margin of error was 3.35% (including a 30% "cluster" effect). The margin of error was exceeded in 37 states and 45 shifted to McCain from the exit poll to the vote. There was a 10.6% difference in margin between the unadjusted exit poll and the recorded vote, far above the 6% discrepancy in 2004.

Uncounted votes are just one factor why Democratic presidential candidates always do better in the unadjusted and preliminary exit polls than the recorded vote. Since the percentage of net uncounted votes has declined steadily since 1988, they are no longer a major factor in causing the discrepancies. Electronic voting has become institutionalized. Touch screen computers (DREs) produce unverifiable results and Optical scanned paper ballots are rarely hand-counted. In addition, the central computers that tabulate total votes for each district/county are vulnerable to malicious programming.

Calculating the True Vote

The first step in calculating the True Vote is to estimate the number of uncounted votes. The Census Bureau surveys total votes cast in every election (the margin of error is less than 0.5%). Key parameters in calculating the True Vote are a) the number of returning voters from the prior election, b) new voters and c) corresponding exit poll vote shares.

In order to calculate a robust estimate of returning voters, we have the mathematical constraint that the number of returning voters must be less than the number who actually voted in the previous election. We need to estimate voter mortality and turnout of prior election voters. An estimated 5% of voters pass on in the four years from the previous election (based on mortality tables). Vote shares are hardly affected by changes in the rate.

The turnout rate of previous election voters still living ("habitual voters") can be estimated from the registered voter turnout. The rate varies from 90-98%, depending on the level of voter interest in the election. It is estimated that in 1992 and 2004, 98% of previous election voters still living turned out to vote due to high voter interest. Of course, the Final National Exit Poll is always forced to match the recorded vote, even if the number of returning voters exceeds the number still living.

We have the simple formulas:
Net Uncounted Vote = Total Votes Cast – Official Recorded Vote
Net Uncounted Vote = Uncounted Votes – Stuffed ballots

Given voter mortality and turnout of living voters from the previous election, we can now calculate an estimate for the number of returning voters. There are 5 calculation methods.

Method 1: Final National Exit Poll: returning voter mix and vote shares are adjusted to match the recorded vote. In 1968, 1988, 1992, 2004 and 2008, the adjusted mix was impossible. It implied over 100% turnout of living Nixon, Bush 1 and Bush 2 voters.

Method 2: Returning voters based on previous election Recorded vote. Calculate the number of new voters in the current election. Note that by calculating returning voters based on total recorded votes, we understate the Democratic vote share, since the calculation does not include heavily Democratic uncounted votes. This method is analogous to the exit pollsters designing a sample based on the previous election voting demographics.

Method 3: Returning voters based on previous election Total Votes Cast with 75% of the uncounted votes assumed to be Democratic
Method 4: Returning voters based on previous election state exit poll aggregate

Method 5: (Recursive. Returning voters based on the previous election True Vote
Returning voters = (Previous Votes Cast * True Vote – voter mortality) * Turnout
New voters = Votes Cast in the current – Returning Voters

This recursive formula applies to all elections:

True Vote (i) = f (Returning Voters (i-1) + New Voters (i))
where i indicates the current election; i-1 is the prior.

The True vote is based on Votes Cast (actual voter intent). But the media only provides the recorded vote.

Prior Election Votes Cast = Recorded Vote + Uncounted Votes
Surviving voters = Votes Cast (Census) - Voter mortality

Current Votes Cast = Surviving Voter Turnout + New Voters

In 2000, 110.9 million votes were cast, 105.4 million recorded with 75% of uncounted votes to Gore1. In 2004, 125.7 million votes were cast, but just 122.3 million recorded. The assumptions: 1.25% annual voter mortality, 98% turnout of living 2000 voters.

Using 12:22am NEP vote shares, Kerry won the True Vote by 10.5 million (53.5-45.2%). He was the winner of all scenarios even assuming a) a 46% Gore vote share (he had a 50.3% True Vote, 49.4% in the unadjusted national exit poll and 48.4% recorded) and b) Kerry had just 89% of returning Gore voters (he had 91% in the 12:22am NEP).

Components of Election Fraud

The True Vote Model is based on National Exit Poll vote shares applied to a feasible mix of returning and new voters. A feature has been added to the model that estimates the number of uncounted, stuffed and switched ballots required to fix the recorded vote – and steal the election.

If NUV is greater than zero, more votes were cast than recorded. Otherwise more votes were recorded than cast (more ballots were stuffed than uncounted). We cannot know how many votes were actually uncounted or stuffed – we only know the net difference.

For instance, if NUV = 200, it could be the result of 300 uncounted and 100 stuffed ballots. Or 400 uncounted and 200 stuffed. If the actual number of uncounted votes were known, the number of stuffed ballots could be calculated. And vice – versa. If the votes are switched in cyberspace, the number of total votes cast is unchanged.

National 2004
Bush won by 62-59 million recorded votes. Kerry won the True vote by 67-57 million. There were 3.44 million net uncounted votes. Estimate 4.40 million uncounted votes.

NUV = Uncounted – Stuffed
Stuffed = 0.96 = 4.40 -3.44

Kerry wins 75% of the 4.4 million uncounted. Assume that 90% of the stuffed ballots were for Bush. Based on these assumptions over 5 million votes were switched from Kerry to Bush.

Ohio 2004
Bush won by 119k recorded votes. Kerry won the unadjusted exit poll by 54.1-45.5% a 500K margin. According to RFK, Jr., there were approximately 350,000 uncounted votes. Assume that 75% (263k) of the uncounted ballots were for Kerry and 86k for Bush. Then there were 143k more votes recorded than cast (143k net stuffed).

Florida
Bush won by 381k recorded votes. Kerry won the unadjusted exit poll by 51.0-48.2%, a 200k margin. There were 238k more votes recorded than cast (238k net stuffed).

New York
A Democratic stronghold, New York afforded a great opportunity for padding the Bush popular vote.
Even though Kerry won the recorded vote by 1.3 million, who has questioned his 58-40% landslide margin?

Kerry's True Vote matched the unadjusted exit poll: 64-35%. The 12% margin discrepancy accounted for nearly 1/3 of Bush's 3 million vote "mandate".

The following estimates are based on the following:
a) Census total votes cast: 75% of uncounted votes were for Kerry
b) 100% of ballot stuffing for Bush.
c) The unadjusted exit polls (Kerry 52.0% state aggregate) are used as the baseline. Kerry's True Vote was close to 53.5%

Again, it is important to note that uncounted votes are estimates. Only the NUV is known. Regardless of the estimate, the final net adjustment is the difference between the recorded and true vote/exit poll. In the final analysis, the discrepancy is known – a combination of uncounted votes, stuffed ballots and switched votes. The combination is a function of the voting system(s).

These states had more votes recorded than cast:
OH, FL, TN, CT, VA and MI.

Florida had 238k net stuffed ballots, Ohio 143k, Tennessee 118k. States with the highest percentage of uncounted ballots:
NM, SC, AL

The 1988-2008 State and National True Vote Model

The model calculates the True Vote for all state and national presidential elections since 1988. It contains a unique database of total state and national votes cast, unadjusted state exit polls and final national exit polls. The TVM has a built-in sensitivity analysis to calculate vote shares and margins over a range of scenarios. It automatically determines vote shares of new and returning voters required to force a match to the state's recorded vote. These capabilities provide a forensic tool to determine the likelihood of vote miscounting in any election.

It is incontrovertible that the Final National Exit Poll (NEP) never reflects the True Vote. The Final is always forced to match the recorded vote even though millions of votes are uncounted in every election. It stands to reason that if the Final is forced to match an impossible recorded vote, then the Final must also be impossible – and therefore all the demographic cross-tabs reported in the media must be invalid.

Simple arithmetic shows that in 1972, 1988, 1992, 2004 and 2008 the number of returning Nixon and Bush voters were not only implausible, but also physically impossible. In 2004 preliminary state and national exit polls were downloaded from the Internet after midnight. They showed Kerry leading by substantial margins.

But final exit polls show that impossible adjustments were made to the number of returning voters ("the mix") as well as to the corresponding vote shares. The reason is obvious, but goes unreported in the mainstream media: It is standard operating procedure to force all exit polls to match the recorded vote – regardless of whether or not the votes were miscounted. Therefore, to obtain a good approximation of the True Vote, the Final NEP returning voter mix must be replaced by a feasible, plausible set based on voter mortality and the best estimated turnout percentage of living previous election voters.

A feasible mix produces a True Vote that is quite close to the unadjusted state and national exit polls. Yet the average Democratic True Vote share usually exceeds the unadjusted exit polls by 1-2%. Why the discrepancy? The exit poll sample is based on prior election recorded votes. But as we know, the recorded vote always differs from the True Vote.

Over 80 million votes were cast but never counted in the eleven presidential elections since 1968. The Republicans led the average recorded vote by 49-45%. The Democrats led the True Vote by exactly the reverse: 49-45%.

The 1988-2008 recorded vote, exit poll and True Vote trends are displayed in tables and a bar graph. Deviations between Democratic and Republican vote shares are indicated, along with the Democratic exit poll discrepancies from the recorded vote.

An additional feature of the model is the reconciliation of True Vote and exit poll discrepancies from the recorded vote. The Net Uncounted Vote (NUV) is the difference between uncounted and stuffed ballots, both of which are usually unknown.

Based on the input uncounted vote rate and the NUV, the number of stuffed ballots and switched votes are calculated.

Four methods are used to calculate a plausible return voter mix. All utilize previous election vote shares adjusted for voter mortality and turnout. The methods determine the number of returning voters based on the following measures:

1 – Official Recorded vote
2 – Votes Cast (recorded + net uncounted)
3 – Unadjusted state exit polls
4 – Recursive True Vote (calculated)

The model has built-in assumptions for the percentage turnout of previous election voters in the current election and allocation of uncounted votes in the previous election. The default assumptions may be overridden. Shares of new and returning voters required to match a given total share are calculated automatically.

In calculating the National True Vote, the model uses Final NEP vote shares. An exception is the 2004 election in which the preliminary 12:22am vote shares are used. As unadjusted "How Voted" exit poll cross-tabs are unavailable for states, the model generates a return voter mix and vote shares that force a match to the recorded vote. The vote shares are derived from the NEP shares by applying a state to national vote share ratio.

Sensitivity Analysis

In 2004, Bush won the recorded vote by 50.7-48.3%. The model shows that Bush needed 109.7% of returning Bush 2000 voters to match his recorded vote.
According to the 12:22am National Exit Poll timeline, Kerry had 57% of new voters, 91.0% of returning Gore voters and 10% of returning Bush voters. In the Final NEP, he had 54%, 90.0% and 9%. The Final was forced to match the recorded vote.

The sensitivity analysis is built-in to the model The first set of tables display 25 scenarios of Kerry vote share, margins and win probabilities. The scenarios are in increments around his base case share: 57% of new voters and 10% share of returning Bush voters.

The second set is based on increments around Kerry's 91% base case share of returning Gore voters and 10% share of new voters. To execute each scenario separately would be prohibitively time-consuming. Note that DNV refers to new voters and others who have voted but not in the previous election.

Results of the first set of scenarios

Worst case: Kerry 53% of DNV; 8% of returning Bush voters
Kerry had 52.1% and a 7.0 million vote margin.
Popular vote win probability: 96.8%

Most likely: Kerry 57% of DNV; 10% of returning Bush voters
Kerry had 53.6% and a 10.7 million vote margin.
Popular vote win probability: 99.8%

Best case: Kerry 61% of DNV; 12% of returning Bush voters
Kerry had 55.1% and a 14.4 million vote margin.
Popular vote win probability: 100.0%

In 1996, Clinton won the unadjusted exit polls (70,000 respondents) by 16 million votes (52.6-37.1%). He had 53.6% in the TVM. His recorded margin was 8 million (49.2-40.8%). The Final National Exit Poll (NEP) was forced to match the recorded vote. There were 10 million uncounted votes. The landslide was denied.

In 2000, Gore won the unadjusted state exit polls (58,000 respondents) by 6 million votes (50.8-44.4%). He had 51.5% in the TVM. But he won the recorded vote by just 540,000. There were 6 million uncounted votes. The election was stolen.

In 2004, Kerry won the unadjusted state exit poll aggregate (76,000 respondents) by 51.1-47.5%. He won the unadjusted National Exit Poll (13,660 respondents) by 51.7-47.0%, a 6 million vote margin. He had 53.6% (a 10 million margin) in the True Vote Model but lost by 3.0 million recorded votes. There were 4 million uncounted votes. The election was stolen.

In 2008, Obama won the unadjusted state exit poll aggregate (83,000 respondents) by 58.1-40.3%, a 23 million vote margin – a near-exact match to the TVM. He won the unadjusted National

Exit Poll (17,836 respondents) by a whopping 61-37%. Officially, he had 52.9% and won by 9.5 million votes. The landslide was denied.

In their 2004 report, the exit pollsters declared that the average 6.5% discrepancy (WPE) in 1250 precincts nationwide was due to the differential response of Kerry and Bush voters to participate in the exit polls. The pollsters hypothesized that 56 Kerry voters responded for every 50 Bush voters – the so-called reluctant Bush responder (rBr) hypothesis. They had no rationale for the hypothesis; they never considered fraud as a reason for the discrepancy.

In fact, rBr was contradicted by survey data which showed that response rates were higher in Bush precincts than Kerry precincts.

The pollsters also claimed that the precinct voting methods did not indicate fraud, but paper ballots had a 2% discrepancy compared to 6-7% for electronic voting (DRE and Optical scanners) and punch card machines. Lever machines precincts had a whopping 11% discrepancy.

The TVM produces sensitivity analysis (5×5 tables) of vote shares, margins and popular vote win probabilities for a range of returning and new voters. The most likely scenario is in the central cell of the table, the worst case is in the lower left cell, and the best case is in the upper right cell.

The win probability is a function of the 2-party vote shares and is calculated using the Normal Distribution Function.

Ohio

At 7:30pm, Kerry was leading the Ohio exit poll by 52.1-47.9% (1963 respondents). He won the unadjusted exit poll (2020 respondents) by 54.1-45.9%.

At 1:41am, the poll flipped to Bush (50.9-48.6%) for the same 2020 respondents, matching the recorded vote. Bush won the recorded vote 50.8-48.7%, a 119,000 vote margin.

Assume 2000 election voters return in proportion to the 2000 unadjusted Ohio exit poll won by Bush (48.5-47.4%). In the Worst Case scenario, Kerry captures 55.7% of new voters and 9.7% of returning Bush 2000 voters. He wins with 52.2%, a 313,000 vote margin and 97.1% win probability.

In the most likely Base Case scenario, Kerry captures 59.5% of new voters and 11.7% of returning Bush 2000 voters. He wins with a 53.7% share, a 480,000 vote margin and a 99.8% win probability.

Florida

At 8:40pm CNN showed a virtual tie. Of 2846 exit polled, Bush led by 49.8-49.7%. Kerry won the unadjusted exit poll (2862 respondents) by 50.8-48.0%. But at 1:41am, the poll flipped to Bush (52.1-47.9%) for the same 2862 respondents, matching the recorded vote. Bush won by a 381,000 recorded vote margin.

Once again, assume that 2000 election voters return in proportion to the 2000 unadjusted Florida exit poll which Gore won by 53.4-43.6%.

In the Worst Case scenario, Kerry captures 52.2% of new voters and 7.5% of returning Bush 2000 voters. Kerry has 53.2% and wins by 569,000 votes with a 99.5% win probability.

In the Base Case scenario, Kerry captures 56.2% of new voters and 9.5% of returning Bush 2000 voters. He has 54.8%, an 800,000 vote margin and 100% win probability.

CHAPTER 7

2010 Midterms

The whole problem with the world is that fools and fanatics are so certain of themselves, but wise people are full of doubt -Bertrand Russell

There was no reason to suspect that the 2010 midterms would be any different than prior elections. The party in power nearly always loses seats in the midterms. But the true number is unknown. The pundits typical reaction promotes the conventional wisdom that it was a GOP blowout of epic proportions – even bigger than 1994.

The unconventional wisdom is that the Democrats virtually always do significantly better than the recorded vote indicates. The 2010 midterms were no exception.

The GOP won the House in a landslide. The Democrats held on to the Senate.

The key question, as usual, was: would Democratic voter turnout overcome the systemic fraud component?

The GOP won gubernatorial elections in FL, OH, PA, WI and NJ (2009). They won the official recorded vote. But did they win the True Vote?

The Democrats led 18 Senate RV polls by 8.5% but only by 1.5% in the corresponding LV polls. The GOP led the latest House Generic LV polls by 6.6% and the RV polls by just 1.2%.

The True Vote Model (TVM) indicates that the Democrats very likely won FL, OH, PA and NJ – and may have won WI. Returning voters are based on the 2008 True Vote, not the recorded vote. A 70% returning McCain voter turnout was assumed, compared to just 62% for returning Obama voters. Obama's True Vote share in the five states was 4.3% higher than his recorded share.

The TVM determines a) a feasible estimate of the breakout of returning voters from the prior election and b) an estimate of vote shares in the current. The number of returning voters is a function of previous election votes cast, voter mortality and estimated turnout.

The 2008 Presidential election is used as the basis for calculating returning voters. The vote shares are derived from the final exit polls. Annual voter mortality is 1.25%.

The number of third-party 2008 voters is given. But the 2010 exit polls indicated that there were more returning third-party voters than were still alive; as we have seen, a common anomaly. According to the Final 2008 National Exit Poll, there were 5 million returning third-party voters – but there were only 1.2 million recorded third-party votes in 2004. Which is correct?

In the 2010 exit polls, returning third-party and new voter percentages are given but corresponding vote shares are N/A. Inquiring minds would like to know why. In order to match the recorded 2010 vote, the GOP candidate had to win 55-60% of new and returning third-party (Other) voters. In the True Vote Model, returning third-party and new voters were assumed to be split equally between the Democrat and the Republican.

Mainstream media pundits never mention the fact that it is standard operating procedure for exit pollsters to force all final national and state exit polls to match the recorded vote. They accept the recorded vote as gospel and never question the official results. But the evidence is overwhelming that in every election, the recorded vote does not equal the True Vote because of systemic election fraud.

The analysis utilizes final likely and registered state and national pre-election polls along with preliminary and final exit polls. The 2010 Midterms Model projected that the final LV pre-election polls would closely match the recorded vote – and they did. Given what we now know about election fraud, what did the final exit polls indicate? They matched the recorded vote. Once again, we had suspicious, unverifiable elections and reluctance of the Democratic leadership to do anything about it.

It must be emphasized that unadjusted exit polls are always forced to match the recorded vote. Late adjustments are made to the exit polls – with no additional respondents. On the other hand, pre-election RV polls have closely matched the unadjusted exit polls. As usual, the pundits quoted the final exit polls as gospel. They warned Obama that he must move to the center – as if he had been part of the "professional left" all along.

Media pundits never questioned the official results. But that is to be expected: they are paid to promote the myth that the recorded vote represents the will of the voters. If they talked about systemic election fraud, they would find themselves out of a job.

Early voting indicated that the Democrats were winning in key races. According to Democratic National Committee (DNC), the Democrats cast more ballots than Republicans in eleven key states, including NV, IA, CA, WI, WA, IL and WV.

The Republican "wave" did not materialize in early voting. District vote history levels (mid-term voters / presidential-year only voters) showed that the Democratic early voting was comparable and often higher than Republican voting. In many key districts, Democrats outpaced Republicans in both ballots cast and participation rates.

Registered and Likely Voter Polls

All pre-election polls interview registered voters. Likely voters are a sub-sample based on the likely voter cutoff model (LVCM). During the last month in every election cycle, the RV samples are replaced by LV subsamples.

Pollsters and media pundits are paid to project the official recorded vote. By utilizing LV polls, they anticipate the election fraud they know is coming. They should project both the recorded and True Vote – but they never mention the fraud factor. They ignore the fact that since 2000, RV projections have closely matched the unadjusted exit polls (i.e. the True Vote).

In 2006 the unadjusted National Exit Poll indicated that the Democrats had a 56.4% share, matching the pre-election RV trend. But the Final NEP was forced to match the 53% recorded share.

The 2010 House and Senate forecast model was based on a comprehensive analysis of Registered Voter (RV) and Likely Voter (LV) polls.

The Senate model used a simulation of the RV and LV polls to forecast average GOP net gains, associated win probabilities and trends. The sensitivity analysis displayed the effects of various undecided voter allocation and vote-switching scenarios.

The House model included a summary comparison of RV and LV Generic polls, win probabilities with a moving average projection. As in the Senate model, the sensitivity analyses displayed the effects of various undecided voter and vote-switching scenario assumptions in forecasting vote shares, House seats and win probabilities. The 2010 summary table illustrated the difference between Rasmussen and other pollsters. The 2006-2010 Generic Poll table provided a historical context.

The model did not assume that LV polls are representative of the electorate. It is true that since the 2000 election, final projections based on likely voter (LV) polls have been quite accurate in predicting the fraudulent recorded vote. while projections based on RV polls have closely approximated the True Vote.

RV polls measure the true intent of the voters – before their votes are hacked by unverifiable voting machines and central tabulators. LV polls predict the miscounted recorded vote. Pollsters and pundits don't dare talk about that.

Polling websites generally displayed only Senate LV polls. CNN/Time provided both RV and LV samples, but only LVs were listed at realclearpolitics.com. The Senate RV forecast model was therefore a mix of RV and LV polls. Without a corresponding RV poll for every LV sub-sample, a pure comparable analysis was difficult.

Unlike the Senate, early House Generic polls were RV samples, except for Rasmussen who only provides LVs. But the pollsters shifted to LVs as Election Day approached.

As expected, the final 2010 National Exit Poll discrepancy from the average of 30 pre-election Generic LV polls was a near-perfect 0.62%. When the returning voter mix was set to the 2008 recorded vote, the discrepancy from the 19 pre-election RV poll average was a miniscule 0.07%.

The final state exit poll (i.e. recorded vote) discrepancy from the average LV poll was 1.5%. When the returning voter mix was set to the 2008 recorded vote, the discrepancy from the RV poll average was an even lower 0.83%.

CNN/Time provided RV and LV polling data for 18 Senate races. Note that RV polls were not listed in the realclearpolitics.com poll averages. Democrats led the RVs in 11 states. They led the LVs in 8 states. They won 9 of the 11 races. Illinois and Pennsylvania flipped from the Democrats in the RV polls to the GOP.

The average GOP LV margin exceeded the RV by 6.3% and the recorded margin by 1.6%.The average GOP recorded margin exceeded the RV by 4.6%. The GOP 4.2% margin exceeded the exit poll by 2.9%.

In the 2006 midterms and 2008 presidential elections, final RV projections gave the Democrats a 7% higher margin than the corresponding LV polls.

Media pundits accept the recorded vote and final exit polls as gospel and never question the official results. And they never mention the fact that it is standard operating procedure for the exit pollsters to force all final national and state exit polls to match the recorded vote.

Historically, the strong correlations between a) pre-election registered voter polls and unadjusted exit polls and b) pre-election likely voter polls and final exit polls (i.e. the recorded vote), is a clear indication of election fraud. We have unverifiable elections and a strange reluctance of the Democratic leadership to do anything about it.

The GOP won the WI, IL and PA senate races. But did they win the True Vote?

All had these factors in common:
1) Progressive candidates (Feingold, Sestak, Giannoulias)
2) Unverifiable DRE voting machines
3) No mandated random hand-counts of optical scanned ballots.
4) The GOP led the final LV polls
5) Democrats led the final RV polls
6) Late exit poll shift to the GOP

Consider the 2010 senate pre-election polls. Based on 37 LV polls (the GOP led the average by 48.1-43.5%), the pre-election model predicted a 50-48 Democratic Senate.

CNN/Time provided RV and LV polling data for 18 Senate races. The Democrats led a combination of 18 RV and 19 LV polls by 45.2-44.6% giving them a 53-45 seat majority. The Democratic RV margin was approximately 5% higher than the LV.

RV polls were not listed in the *realclearpolitics.com* final polling averages. The Democrats led the average RV poll by 49.2-40.6%. They also led the corresponding LVs by 46.6-45.8%. The Democratic margin was 8% higher in the RV polls.

2010 Adjusted National Exit Poll

The final indicated that 45% of the electorate were returning Obama voters and 45% were McCain voters. Obama's recorded vote margin was 52.9-45.6%. Of course, the pundits will claim that the 7.3% discrepancy was due to millions of unenthusiastic Democrats who did not return to vote in 2010.

The pollsters make adjustments to the number of returning voters (the "mix") and the vote shares in order to match the vote count. Obama won the recorded vote by 9.5 million, but his True Vote margin was at least twice that. His recorded share understated his True vote share by 4-5%.

If the 2010 NEP returning voter mix is adjusted to match the 2008 recorded share (53-45%), the average Democratic share is within

1% of the GOP share – and matches the pre-election RV polls. The adjusted 53% Democratic share of the 2010 electorate is 5% lower than Obama's True share.

The Democrats were expected to lose seats in the Senate and House. They were surely going to lose in Arkansas. They were expected to hold on to CA, WA, WV, NY, DE and OR. And they did. The IL, NV, PA, CO and WI elections were expected to be close. And they were. The Democrats won NV and CO. But they lost WI, IL and PA. Or did they? Oregon could hold the answer.

The Democrats won in states that had 100% paper ballots (OR, WA) which mandated random hand recounts or encouraged vote by mail (CO, CA). But WI, PA and IL voted by machine. The GOP won those states.

The Oregon senate race was never in question. Wyden led by a consistent 20% in the pre-election LV polls. He had a 57% recorded share – just as the polls predicted, matching Obama's share in 2008. But if Oregon reflects the national electorate, how does one explain the GOP 52-47% House Generic margin in 2010?

Once again, just as in 2004, the Battleground states shifted to the GOP – except for Oregon. Was it because Oregon mandates random full hand-counts of the optically-scanned paper ballots to check the central tabulator machine-counts?

Washington now votes virtually 100% by mail. Colorado and California also had a high percentage of mail-in paper and absentee ballots. Is it a coincidence that in these states, the Democrats won by margins equivalent to Obama in 2008?

Ohio
Kasich (Rep) won by 77,000 votes (49.8-47.8%).
Strickland (Dem) won the exit poll: 49.9-47.4% (101,000).
Strickland won the True Vote by 338,000 (52.2%).
If Strickland had 81% of Obama voters and 11% of McCain's, he wins by 51,000.

Pennsylvania
Corbett (Rep) won by 357,000 recorded votes.
Corbett won the unadjusted exit poll: 54.3-45.3%.

If Onorato (Dem) had 83% of Obama voters and 8% of McCain, he wins by 83,000.

Wisconsin
Walker (Rep) won by 105,000 recorded votes (52-47%).
Walker won the unadjusted exit poll: 52.4-46.0%.
If Barrett (Dem) had 87% of Obama voters and 7% of McCain, he wins by 28,000.

New Jersey
Christie (Rep) won by 99,000 votes (48.7-45.6%).
If Corzine (Dem) had 77% of Obama voters and 7% of McCain, he wins by 76,000.

CHAPTER 8

Recall Wisconsin

All truth passes through three stages. First, it is ridiculed. Second, it is violently opposed. Third, it is accepted as self-evident.
- Arthur Schopenhauer

Wisconsin became the epicenter of election activism in April 2011 as a result of the disputed Supreme Court recount and by irregularities in the state senate and governor recall elections. Election activists have come to see this historically progressive state become a poster child of election fraud, joining Ohio and Florida.

I became an early member of several Wisconsin Election Integrity groups and have created True Vote Models and various statistical analyses for the 2011 Supreme Court election, state senate recall elections and citizen exit polls.

In 2012, there were more than one million signed petitions to recall Governor Walker. I did an extensive pre and post-election analyses of the recall.

The analysis determined that fraud was very likely in virtually all of these special elections. The models were confirmed by physical evidence of anomalies in the chain of ballot custody and the astounding refusal of the Wisconsin Government Accounting Board (GAB) to cooperate with activists who were investigating a) the security of the ballots, b) use of unverifiable touch screen computers, c) software controlled by third-parties ("Command Central") and d) GAB refusing to allow public viewing of voting records.

The Supreme Court Election

Kloppenburg, the Independent candidate, was the apparently winner. But 14,000 ballots were "found" in Waukesha County shortly after the election. Prosser, the Republican, was declared the unofficial winner by 7,000 votes. The subsequent recount was a travesty. Scores of slit ballot bags were photographed. Poll tapes were found dated a week before the election. A stack of 50 consecutive Prosser ballots were found in the Town of Verona in Dane County where Kloppenburg had 67% of the recorded vote.

The Wisconsin True Vote Model was predicated on a feasible estimate of returning voters from the prior election and an estimate of voter shares in the current election. The model showed that Kloppenburg very likely won the election.

The number of returning voters is a function of prior election total votes cast, voter mortality and estimated turnout. The 2008 Presidential True Vote was used as the basis for calculating returning voters. New voters were assumed to be split equally between Kloppenburg and Prosser. New voters were calculated as follows:

Total Votes = returning 2008 voter turnout + New 2010 voters
New 2010 voters = 2010 vote – returning 2008 voters

Assuming a 50% turnout of Obama and McCain voters, the recorded vote implied that Kloppenburg had just 81% of returning Obama voters while Prosser had 93% of returning McCain voters. The model showed that if Kloppenburg had 88% of Obama voters and 50% of 70,000 returning third-party and new voters, she would have won by approximately 100,000 votes with a 53% vote share.

Sensitivity analysis tables for Wisconsin, Milwaukee and Waukesha counties displayed vote shares and margins for 25 turnout and vote share scenario combinations.

In Milwaukee County, Obama had 67.3%, Kloppenburg won by just 29,700 recorded votes with 56.4%. Obama had a 36% margin compared to just 13% for Kloppenburg. In order to match the recorded vote, assuming equal 50% Obama and McCain voter turnout, Prosser had to win 20% of Obama voters and 95% of McCain voters.

Are we to believe that Prosser won 1 out of 5 returning Obama voters? If we assume that Kloppenburg had 90% of Obama voters, then she won by 61,000 votes with a 63% share. One must conclude that election fraud cut Kloppenburg's margin in Milwaukee County by approximately 31,000 votes.

Prosser won Waukesha County by 59,500 votes, a 73.8-26.2% margin (Obama had 37.7%). In order to match the recorded vote, Prosser needed 35% of Obama voters and 97% of McCain voters (assuming equal 55% voter turnout).

Are we expected to believe that more than 1 in 3 Obama voters defected to Prosser? On the other hand, if we assume that Kloppenburg had 90% of Obama voters, election fraud inflated Prosser's Waukesha margin by around 23,000 votes.

Senate Recalls

The True Vote model indicated that only election fraud could keep the Democrats from winning at least three of three of the six GOP state senate recall elections. They won two. A post-election analysis indicates that they did much better. They may very well have won all six.

The Democrats won 5 of the total 9 recall elections vote with a 50.5% share. In 2008, Obama won the 9 districts with a 54.5% share. The Republicans won 4 of the 6 GOP districts with 55.2%. Obama had 51.5% in the four districts.

There had to be an implausibly low returning Obama voter turnout and/or an implausibly high defection of Obama voters. The Democrats did 3.2% better than Obama in the three Democratic recalls, but 5.4% worse in the 6 GOP recalls, an implausible difference.

These anomalies, combined with documented evidence of voting irregularities and massive exit poll discrepancies, were very strong indicators of Election Fraud. It is very likely that the Democrats won at least seven of the nine elections.

In the GOP districts, voter turnout was 65% of the 2008 presidential election and just 48% in the Democratic districts.

Assuming zero net defection, approximately 58% of Obama voters and 85% of McCain voters turned out - an implausible difference. Assuming equal 65% turnout, the Democrats won 82% of Obama voters and Republicans won 92% of McCain voters – an implausible 10% net Obama defection.

The Democrats won two GOP districts with an average 53.2% share, Obama had 55.9%. Total turnout was 66%. Approximately 63% of Obama voters turned out. That is plausible. Assuming equal turnout, the Democrats won 91% of Obama voters and 5% of McCain voters. That is very plausible.

The three Democratic recall elections were landslides in which they had a 58.8% aggregate share. Obama had 55.5%. Approximately 48% of 2008 voters turned out. Assuming zero net defection, 52% were Obama voters and 44% McCain. That is plausible. Assuming equal 48% turnout, the Democrats won 98% of Obama and 8% of McCain voters (6% net McCain defection). That is also plausible.

In any election, there are two key factors: voter turnout and voter preference. We know how many voters returned from the previous election (as a percentage). But we must estimate the percentage mix of returning Democrats and Republicans.

The number of new voters is just the difference between total votes cast in the current election and returning voters. In the recall analysis, we will assume that new voters were split equally between the Democrats and the Republicans.

The Democrats were highly motivated to win the Senate based on Walker policies, but the GOP had the advantage of massive funding – especially in District 8. The problem was to determine voter turnout rates and preferences that were required to match the recorded vote.

Obama won each of the six districts by a 53.0-45.7% margin. Therefore assuming a) an equal percentage turnout of Obama and McCain voters and b) no changes in voter preference, the Democrats would win all six elections (see below).

But since the GOP won four, there had to be a higher turnout rate of McCain voters than Obama voters and/or a net defection of Obama voters to the GOP.

In the first set of calculations, we reasonably assume that a) 60% of McCain voters turned out in the recalls and b) there was zero net defection (Democrats won 95% of returning Obama voters and the GOP won 95% of returning McCain voters). In order to match the average recorded vote, Obama turnout had to be 45% compared to 60% for McCain.

In the second set, we assume that a) 60% of McCain voters and 60% of Obama voters turned out and the GOP won 95% of returning McCain voters, but b) there were net defections of Obama voters to the GOP. In order to match the average recorded vote, the average Democratic share of Obama voters had to be approximately an unlikely 83%.

The two sets of scenarios are implausible.

In District 2, if 60% of McCain voters turned out, then just a minuscule 33% of Obama voters turned out (assuming zero net defection of Obama and McCain voters). Assuming equal 60% turnout of Obama and McCain voters, there had to be a massive net 25% defection of Democrats from Obama to McCain.

In District 8, if 60% of McCain voters turned out, then just 47% of Obama voters turned out (assuming zero net defection). Assuming equal 60% Obama and McCain turnout, there was a 10% net defection of Democrats from Obama to McCain. Therefore, Pasch won assuming equal turnout and zero net defection.

District 18 was won by King, the Democrat. Obama's required 58% turnout nearly matched McCain's 60% (assuming zero net defection). Assuming equal 60% turnout, there was a tiny 1% net defection to McCain.

District 32 was won by the Democrats. Since Obama had 61%, it would have raised eyebrows if the Democrats lost. A low 47% Obama turnout was required to match the Democratic 55.4% vote share. Assuming equal 60% turnout, the required 8% net defection to McCain is reasonable. The numbers show that Shilling won.

For the Democrats to win all six elections:
a) Obama voter turnout (60%) had to match McCain.
b) Democrats had 93% of Obama and 5% of McCain voters (maximum 2% defection)
c) Democrats needed an average 52.3% share. Obama had 53.7% in the six districts, but probably did 4-5% better since he had 63% in the Wisconsin exit poll and 56% recorded.

Citizen Exit Polls

In each of the five Citizen Exit Polls conducted in two Wisconsin districts, the Democrats did much better than the official count (67.8% vs. 52.4% on average). Why the large discrepancies? Are the polls to be believed? This analysis provides a possible explanation, keeping in mind that it is based on a limited number of exit poll locations.

It is important to understand the difference between the Wisconsin Citizen exit polls and corporate sponsored state and national exit polls. The Citizen polls had a very simple aim: to compare how respondents said they voted to the official count.

In three strong Democratic recall locations, Democratic exit poll shares (78.8%) were significantly higher than the vote counts (66.9%). Shorewood was 10.9% higher, Pardeeville 8.5% and Baraboo 15.8%. The True Vote Model (TVM) closely matched the recorded votes. Overall voter participation was 52%.

If the vote counts were correct, 61% of Democrats and 33% of Republicans responded. Republican voters may have been reluctant to respond in these heavily Democratic locations. If that was the case, then the exit polls overstated the True Democratic vote.

In the two strong Republican locations (Butler and Menomonee Falls), the Democrats had 43.1% in the exit polls compared to 31.5% in the count (16.5% higher in Butler, 11.0% in Menomonee). In the TVM, the Democrats did 11.0% and 8.3% better, respectively. Overall just 33% of voters participated.

If the vote counts were correct, then 45% of Democrats and 28% of Republicans responded – an implausible Democratic participation in these strong GOP locations. Therefore, it is likely that the votes were miscounted and the exit polls were close to the True Vote.

The aggregate Democratic True Vote share was 55.2%, a close match to the 55.5% aggregate share based on equal Democratic and Republican response in each location. The discrepancies could have been due to a COMBINATION of vote miscounts and differential response rates.

Assuming EQUAL Democratic and Republican response rates, Democratic shares were 73.0% (6.1% higher than recorded) in Democratic locations and 35.4% in Republican locations (3.9% higher).

Exit Poll Response Required to Match Recorded Vote

The Democratic exit poll response rate was 57%; the Republican rate was 30%. Democratic response exceeded Republican response in each of the five locations. But what if the overall Republican response was also 57%? What would the response rate have to be in each location for the exit poll to match the 52.4% Democratic share?

The required Republican rate was derived using the Excel Solver algorithm. The Democratic rate was held constant to the actual exit poll. Republican response was constrained to exceed Democratic response in Menomonee Falls and Butler. The required response rates were not plausible. Republican response exceeded the Democrats in 4 of the 5 locations (including Democratic strongholds Pardeeville and Shorewood).

Exit Poll Refusal Rates

Exit Poll refusal is the difference between the total number of non-responders and the number of non-responders required to match the recorded vote. The refusal rate is the ratio of refusals to the recorded vote.

The average Republican refusal rate in Democratic locations was 18.8%: Baraboo 16.6%, Pardeeville 12.9% and Shorewood 22.5%. In Republican locations, the rate was 5.6%: Menomonee Falls 5.9%, Butler 5.2%. Republican voters were four times more likely to refuse an exit poll interview in Democratic than in Republican locations.

Based on the True Vote Model and the exit polls, it is very likely that the District 8 and 14 recall elections were stolen. The Republican 17-16 majority should be an 18-15 majority for the Democrats.

The True Vote Model requires an estimate of the True Vote in the previous election in order to determine a plausible mix of returning voters. In 2008, Obama had a 56.2% recorded vote share in Wisconsin, but he had 63.3% in the unadjusted exit poll. The margin of error was 2.4% (including a 30% cluster effect) for 2545 respondents.

Using a miscounted recorded vote from the previous election as a basis for forecasting or post-election analysis will produce a fraudulent result in the current election.

These were the base case assumptions used in the TVM:
1) Equal percentage turnout of Obama/McCain voters.
2) Democrats win 95% of returning Obama voters; Republicans win 95% of McCain.
3) Democrats and Republican new voter shares are proportional to the 2008 vote.

A sensitivity analysis table displayed Democratic vote shares for each location based on nine scenario combinations of returning Obama and McCain voters. The base case scenario is the central cell of the 3×3 table.

The Walker Recall

The exit pollster's MO never changes. In the recall, the pundits said it was "too close to call". Barrett was probably winning, but the media knew the fix was in so they had to keep it close. They also knew the actual exit poll numbers would not see the light of day. So they called the election quickly for Walker.

Barrett should have won – assuming ZERO fraud. In 2008, Obama had a 56.2% recorded vote share in Wisconsin, but he had 63.2% in the unadjusted exit poll (2,545 respondents). The poll had a 2.43% margin of error (including a 30% "cluster effect"). The probability was nearly 100% that Obama's True Wisconsin share exceeded 60%. The following scenarios assume he had 60%.

I. Base Case assumptions (favoring Walker)
Returning 2008 Voter Turnout:
Obama 65%, McCain 75%
Barrett wins 90% of Obama and 5% of returning McCain voters
Result: Barrett wins by 54.6-45.4% (198,000 votes)
Walker needs to flip 8% of Barrett votes to win.

II. Zero Net Turnout and Voter Defection Scenarios
1. Equal 70% Turnout
Barrett wins 90% of Obama and 5% of McCain voters
Result: Barrett has 56.2% and wins by 267,000 votes.
Walker needs to flip 11% to win.

2. Equal 70% Turnout
Barrett wins 95% of Obama and 5% of McCain voters.
Result: Barrett has 59% and wins by 387,000 votes.
Walker needs to steal 15% to win.

III. Democratic Worst Case Scenarios
1. Voter Turnout: 65% of Obama; 70% of McCain

Barrett wins 85% of Obama voters and 0% of McCain voters.
Result: Barrett has 50.2% and wins by 9,000 votes.
2. Voter Turnout: 60% Obama; 75% McCain
Barrett wins 90% of Obama voters and 5% of McCain voters.
Result: Barrett has 51.8% and wins by 80,000 votes.

IV. Implausible Scenarios
1. Voter Turnout: 55% Obama; 80% McCain
Barrett wins 90% of Obama voters and 5% of McCain voters.
Result: Barrett has 49.1% and loses by 38,000.

2. Voter Turnout: 65% Obama; 70% McCain
Barrett wins 80% of Obama voters and 5% of McCain voters.
Result: Barrett has 49.4% and loses by 25,000.

Was the Past Prologue?

The True Vote Model indicated that Barrett would win a fair election with 53-54%.

Approximately 69% of 2008 voters turned out. Walker defeated Barrett by 125,000 recorded votes (52.2-46.6%).

What did it take for Walker to win in 2010?

In order to match the recorded vote, the exit poll required that 49% of the 2010 electorate were returning Obama voters and 43% returning McCain. The 6% spread was 8% below Obama's recorded margin and a whopping 22% below his exit poll margin. The spread implies that 66% of Obama voters and 77% of McCain voters returned in 2010 – a net 11% turnout advantage to Walker.

The exit poll indicated that Barrett had 83% of returning Obama voters and 7% of McCain - a net 10% Obama voter defection. Walker had 16% of Obama voters and 93% of McCain. In addition, 3% were returning third-party and 5% did not vote in 2008. Strangely, the corresponding vote shares were listed as N/A. A simple calculation shows that Walker needed to win new and returning third-party voters by a 20% margin.

To summarize, in order to match the recorded vote, the adjusted Final 2010 Wisconsin exit poll assumed 1) ZERO fraud in the 2008 election, 2) McCain returning voter turnout exceeded Obama turnout by 11%, 3) 16% of Obama voters defected to Walker and 7% of McCain defected to Barrett, 4) Walker had a 20% margin among new and returning 2008 third-party voters.

The base case assumption in the 2012 Wisconsin Recall True Vote Model is that Obama had a 60% vote share. He had 56.2% recorded, far below his 63.3% exit poll share (2545 respondents).

Given the 2.4% margin of error, the probability is virtually 100% that Obama's True Vote share exceeded 60%. The discrepancy is a very strong indicator that Obama did much better than his 56% official share and the Wisconsin 2008 election was fraudulent.

Unlike final national and state exit polls that are adjusted to conform to the recorded vote and implicitly assume zero fraud, the True Vote Model is based on a feasible estimated turnout of previous election voters and best vote share estimates of returning and new voters. The model calculated various scenarios ("sensitivity analysis") of 2008 voter turnout in 2012 based on the 2008 recorded vote, unadjusted exit poll and estimated True Vote. What did this portend for the recall? There are three scenarios:

1) Fraud: Walker wins by a similar margin (125,000) as in 2010.
2) Fraud: But not enough to steal. Barrett wins by 70,000.
3) No fraud. Barrett wins by at least 160,000.

Before the first votes were posted, the media reported that based on the exit polls, the election was "too close to call". But Walker won by 53.2-46.3%, a 173,000 vote margin. There was a significant 7% discrepancy between the unadjusted exit poll and the recorded vote. What caused the red shift?

The Wisconsin exit poll (2547 respondents) indicated that Walker had 53.0%. The 0.2% difference between the Final and the recorded vote was the result of the standard policy of forcing the unadjusted poll to match the vote.

The pollsters claimed that the exit poll had a 4.0% margin of error. But they could not have meant the adjusted poll because it is always forced to match the recorded vote to within 0.5%. Why did the media not provide the unadjusted exit poll crosstabs? Was it because they knew that they would have to adjust all the crosstabs to match a bogus recorded vote and did not want the public to view the "adjustments"?

The Fraud Factor

There was no mention of the fraud factor in the mainstream media. There never is. To the exit pollsters and the media, there is no such thing as election fraud. The GOP employed overt voter disenfranchisement in plain sight by robo- calling voters with false information and telling voters to use unverifiable touch screen DREs rather than paper ballots. But the media never considered that right-wing voting machine programmers would write malicious code to covertly flip votes in cyberspace.

In 2010, Walker "won" by 52.2-46.6%, supposedly due to low-Democratic turnout. But the Democrats turned out heavily in the recall. There was no way that Walker could match his 2010 vote – if the votes were counted as cast. But that is a quaint notion considering the overwhelming evidence of systemic election fraud since 1988.

Implausible 2008 returning voters and 2012 vote shares

Obama had a 56.2% recorded share in Wisconsin and 63.3% in the unadjusted exit poll (2.4% margin of error). Assuming Obama had a 60% True Vote share, then to match the recall vote, Walker needed an 81% turnout of McCain and 71% turnout of Obama voters; he needed 25% of Obama voters, 95% of McCain and 46% of new voters. The 2012 exit poll indicates he had 45% of new voters who comprised 13% of the total vote.

In order to win by his recorded vote, Walker needed a 10% advantage in returning 2008 voters and a 20% advantage in net defections. That is highly implausible.

The True Vote Model indicates that Barrett should have won easily – assuming the election was fair.

Consider these exit poll anomalies:

1) 5% of voters were not white or black. The shares were n/a.
2) Philosophy: 13% of liberals voted for Walker.
3) Party ID: 34% Democrat/35% Republican in a progressive state.
4) Labor: Only 62% voted for Barrett.
5) Obama preferred by 51-44% but Barrett lost by 53.2-46.3%.
6) Barrett had just 81% of would-be Obama voters.
7) 2010 voter turnout: Walker: 47-34%. He "won" in 2010 by 5.6%.
8) Urban vote: Barrett had just 62% in big cities.

The pollsters indicate that there were 2547 exit poll respondents and the margin of error (MoE) was +/-4%. Presumably, this includes a 30% cluster factor. But it was too high considering the number of respondents. The calculated margin of error was just 2.6% (including a 30% cluster factor).

If we had unadjusted exit poll data, the margin of error could be applied to determine the confidence interval where the vote shares would be expected to fall 95% of the time. That is why unadjusted exit polls are necessary. The standard practice of forcing the exit poll to match the recorded vote implicitly assumes zero fraud.

This analysis uses the Wisconsin Recall True Vote Model (TVM) to calculate Walker's share of Obama returning voters that were required to match the state/county recorded vote. It is further evidence that Walker's recorded margin was implausible and that Barrett very likely won the election.

Walker won in 2010 by 124,638 votes with a 52.3% share. His margin improved in 2012 to 171,105 votes and a 53.1% share.

In the recall Walker's greatest vote margins (in thousands) were in these counties: Waukesha (96), Washington (36), Brown (21), Ozaukee (20) and Outagamie (18). His greatest percentage margin increases were in Taylor, Trempealeau, Price, Outagamie and Clark.

The highest vote gains were in Waukesha, Milwaukee, Outagamie, Brown and Dane.

Obama won Wisconsin with a 56.2% recorded share. But he had 63.3% in the unadjusted exit poll. It's strong evidence that fraud sharply reduced his True Vote. The recorded vote was used as a conservative basis to calculate returning voters, so the following results are probably inflated for Walker.

The sensitivity analysis tables display vote shares and margins over a range of 2008 voter turnout and vote share assumptions. The base case assumptions were:
1) Equal 85% turnout of Obama and McCain voters.
2) Equal 50% Barrett and Walker share of new voters.
3) Barrett won 5% of returning McCain voters

Wisconsin
Obama had 56.2%.
Walker had 52.9% and won by 171,000 votes.
Walker needed 22% of returning Obama voters.
If Barrett had 90% of Obama voters, he wins by 168,000 votes with a 53.3% share.

Waukesha
Obama had 36.4%.
Walker had 72.4% and won by 96,082 votes.
Walker needed 42% of returning Obama voters.
If Barrett had 90% of Obama voters, Walker wins a 61.9% share.

Racine
Obama had 53.1%.
Walker had 52.7% and won by 5,857 votes.
Walker needed 17% of returning Obama voters.
If Barrett had 90% of Obama voters, he wins a 50.7% share.

Brown
Obama had 53.9%.
Walker had 59.7% and won by 20,160 votes.
Walker needed 31% of returning Obama voters.
If Barrett had 90% of Obama voters, he wins a 51.4% share.

Jefferson

Obama had 49.7%.

Walker had 60.6% and won by 7,777 votes.

Walker needed 27% of returning Obama voters.

If Barrett had 90% of Obama voters, Walker wins 51.4%.

Marathon

Obama won with a 53.5% share.

Walker had 62.4% and won by 14,543 votes.

Walker needed 37% of returning Obama voters.

If Barrett had 90% of Obama voters, he wins a 51.2% share.

Crawford

Obama had 62.5%.

Walker had 51.0% and won by 197 votes.

Walker needed 27% of returning Obama voters.

If Barrett had 90% of Obama voters, he wins with 59.0%.

Outagamie

Obama had 54.5%.

Walker had 61.3% and won by 18,126 votes.

Walker needed 36% of returning Obama voters.

If Barrett had 90% of Obama voters, he wins with 52.4%.

Milwaukee

Obama had 67.3%.

Barrett had 62.5% and won by 107,021 votes.

Barrett needed 91% of Obama voters.

Dane

Obama had 72.83%.

Barrett had 69.1% and won by 98,812 votes

Barrett needed 95% of Obama voters.

The Walker Recall County/Ward Database was created to facilitate analysis. The data was made available as an Excel spreadsheet from the Wisconsin GAB and consists of 3500 Ward vote records.

Barrett won all sensitivity analysis scenarios with shares of returning Obama voters ranging from 84-90%. Obama's vote share ranged from his 56.2% recorded to the 63.3% exit poll share.

The assumptions were a) equal 85% turnout of Obama and McCain voters and b) Barrett had 5% of McCain voters. Barrett had 50.3% in the worst case scenario and 59.6% in the best case.

Winnebago County

Winnebago had both Optical scanners and Touch screens in a number of voting locations. In a given voting location, one would expect the corresponding vote shares to be nearly equal. But if they aren't, we need to calculate the probability that the discrepancy is due to chance.

The probabilities were based on the recorded votes for both machine types and are a function of a) the number of votes on the optical scanners and touch screens and b) the corresponding vote share percentages.

If we know the number of votes cast on the optical scanners, we can calculate the number of touch screen votes and vote shares.

Assume that in a given location,
nv = total number of votes,
ns = number of optical scan ballots (hand count)
ps = Walker's percentage on optical scanners (hand count)
nt = number of touch screen votes = $nv - ns$
pt = Walker's percentage on touch screens (calculated)

The Z-score is based on the bell-curve (normal distribution). Z determines the probability of the difference between the touch screen and optical scan vote shares.

If $Z = 1.65$, the probability is 95.2% that the difference between the touch screen and optical scan vote shares was not due to chance.
For $Z = 1.96$, the probability is 97.5%.
If $Z = 2.33$, the probability is 99.0%.

The probability of the difference in vote shares is calculated:
1) Difference between Walker's touch screen and scanner shares:
Diff = pt-ps

2) Standard error of the proportions:
Std = sqrt [ps * (1-ps)/ns + pt * (1-pt)/nt]

3) The Z-score: Z = Diff / Std

4) Probability = normsdist (Z)

The low probabilities in the following locations could not have been due to chance.

Location	Walker	ns	nt	ps	pt	Z	Probability
Village of Poygan	66.6%	255	186	63.9%	70.7%	1.84	3.3%
Village of Rushford	61.8%	262	207	58.5%	65.9%	1.66	4.9%
Village of Utica	68.6%	380	109	66.7%	75.3%	1.77	3.8%
Village of Neenah	63.5%	112	741	63.1%	73.2%	1.43	7.7%
City of Neenah (17-20)	52.5%	761	75	51.3%	64.1%	2.19	1.2%
City of Oshkosh (17)	42.6%	272	112	40.5%	47.7%	1.29	9.9%
City of Oshkosh (28A)	46.8%	317	102	45.0%	52.6%	1.34	9.0%
City of Oshkosh (29A)	63.8%	174	56	60.6%	73.7%	1.88	3.0%

Voting Machine Correlation Analysis

The purpose of the correlation analysis was to determine the effect of paper ballots, touch screens (DRE) and optical scanners on vote shares. The source of the data was the *Wisconsin Government Accounting Board Form 190- Voting by Type of Equipment.*

There was a negative (-.24) correlation between Barrett's county vote shares and corresponding percentage of total votes cast on DREs. Overall Barrett did better on paper ballots (0.11 correlation) and optical scanners (0.14). As the percentage of votes cast on DREs increased, so did Walker's vote shares.

Of the 59 counties that Walker won, 54 used touch screens (DREs), but the majority of votes were cast on optical scanners. In the 13 counties that Barrett won, just five had DREs.

These were the DRE percentages of the total vote in Barrett counties: Iowa (76%), Eau Claire (21%), Kenosha (12%), Columbia (0.2%) and Milwaukee (0.5%). The number of DREs was negligible in counties that Barrett won.

Several correlations were calculated. The first set was to determine if there was a relationship between the municipal vote shares and the percentage of DRE votes cast in each municipality.

The correlations between the percentage of votes cast by machine type and county vote size was a strong 0.45. The correlations were negative for DREs (-0.41) and paper (-0.31). DREs and paper ballots were mostly used in smaller counties.

Correlation ratios measured the strength of the relationship between voting machines and county vote shares. Voters were encouraged to use DRE's rather than paper ballots.

In the counties Walker won, Barrett's vote shares were positively correlated to the percentage of paper ballots (.20) and votes cast on DREs (0.17). His shares were negatively correlated to optical scanners (-0.21).

CHAPTER 9

Obama and the Fraud Factor

Men occasionally stumble over the truth, but most of them get themselves up and hurry off as if nothing happened - Winston Churchill

The 2012 Presidential True Vote and Election Fraud Simulation Model (TVM) is a combination of the pre-election Monte Carlo Simulation Election Model, based on the latest state polling; and the True Vote Model, based on a feasible estimate of new and returning 2008 voters and corresponding estimated vote shares. The model is updated weekly for the latest state and national polls.

Based on the historic record, Obama needs at least 55% to overcome the systemic built-in fraud factor in 2012. In 2008 Obama had a 58-40.5% weighted average in the unadjusted state exit polls (82,000 respondents)). He won the unadjusted National Exit Poll (17,836 respondents) by a whopping 61-37%.

The 2008 True Vote Model was confirmed by the exit polls. It determined that Obama had a 58% share, exactly matching the state exit poll aggregate.

But mainstream media websites (Fox, CNN, ABC, CBS, NYT, etc.) still show that Obama had 52.9% – for the same 17,836 NEP respondents. As always, the FINAL National Exit poll was forced to match the recorded share.

The exit pollsters have never explained the massive 11% state exit poll margin discrepancy, much less the impossible 17% National Exit Poll. If they ever do so, they will surely claim that the anomalies were due to flawed polling samples. *But how could the exit polls be so much farther off than they were in 2004?*

The media has never explained why in at least four presidential elections, forcing the exit polls to match the recorded vote required impossible weighting adjustments.

Media pundits and pollsters project the recorded vote – and they are usually right. They know there will be fraud, so they prepare you for it. The RV polls are transformed to LVs to promote an artificial "horse race". The pundits want to predict the recorded vote. The closer they are, the better they look. But they never mention that it's the fraud factor that gets them close.

The scenarios are based on the 2008 True Vote. Pollsters, academics and media pundits do not consider or mention the True Vote and rigged voting machines. It's not in their vocabulary. They can't mention one without the other. They base all pre-election and post-election analysis on the recorded vote.

The 2012 model projects state and national votes. Turnout rates and vote shares used in projecting the national shares are applied in each state in order to derive the national aggregate. A 1.25% annual voter mortality rate is assumed.

The TVM has two options for estimating returning voters. The True Vote (default) option assumes that 2008 voters return in proportion to the unadjusted exit poll aggregate (Obama by 58-40.5%). In this scenario, Obama wins in 2012 by 55-45% with 371 EV. He has a virtual 100% EV win probability.

The Recorded Vote option assumes that 2008 voters return in proportion to the 2008 recorded vote (Obama 52.9-45.6%). As of mid-September polling, the model has Obama winning the recorded vote by 52-48% with 310 EV. He has a 96% win probability.

The TVM displays the effects of turnout rates and shares of returning voters. Three tables are generated for nine scenario combinations of Obama and McCain turnout rates and shares of returning Obama and McCain voters. The tables provide resulting vote shares, margins and popular vote win probabilities.

Two forecasting methods are used in the model. The TVM projects state vote shares based on estimated shares of new and returning voters; the Monte Carlo 500 election trial simulation uses state pre-election polls. The electoral vote win probability is the number of winning election trials divided by 500.

The projected state vote share is the poll plus the undecided voter allocation (UVA).

The model uses state vote share projections as input to the Normal Distribution function to determine the state win probability.

Just like in the 2004 and 2008 simulations, a random number (RND) between 0 and 1 is generated for each state and compared to Obama's state win probability.

If RND is greater than the win probability, Romney wins the state. If RND is less than the win probability, Obama wins.

The winner of the election trial is the candidate who has at least 270 electoral votes. The process is repeated for 500 election trials.

Electoral Votes and Win Probabilities

The Electoral Vote is calculated in three ways.

1. The snapshot EV is a simple summation of the state electoral votes. It could be misleading since there may be several very close elections which go one way.

2. The Theoretical EV is the product sum of the electoral votes and win probabilities. A simulation or meta-analysis is not required to calculate the expected EV.

3. The Mean EV is the average electoral vote in the 500 simulated elections.

As the number of election trials increase, the Mean EV approaches the Theoretical EV, illustrating the Law of Large Numbers. The snapshot EV will differ slightly from the Theoretical EV, depending on the number of closely contested states.

Obama's electoral vote win probability is his winning percentage of the 500 simulated election trials. The national popular vote win probability, like those of individual states, is calculated by the normal distribution using the aggregate of the projected state vote shares. The aggregate margin of error is 1-2% lower than the MoE of the individual states.

Obama needs at least a 55% True Vote share to win in 2012 if, as in 2008, he loses 5% due to fraud.

The combination of True Vote Model and state poll-based Monte Carlo Simulation is useful to determine if the electoral and popular vote share estimates are reasonable; state and national pre-election polls are compared to the TVM.

The TVM can be forced to match the aggregate pre-election poll projection by adjusting the vote shares, mimicking the exit pollsters procedure of forcing unadjusted polls to match the recorded vote, A red flag would be raised if the match required that Obama captured just 85% of returning Obama voters while Romney wins 95% of returning McCain voters (a 10% net defection).

If McCain voter turnout is 10-15% higher than Obama in order to match the vote, it would also raise a red flag.

Setting the returning voter option to the 2008 recorded vote implies that the 2008 election was fraud-free (i.e. recorded vote was the True Vote). We know the election was highly fraudulent, but media and academic election forecasters ignore the fraud factor. The resulting vote shares will closely match the LV polls and suggest that Romney has a good chance of winning a rigged election.

In 2008, Obama had a 52.9% recorded vote share. Using the recorded share as a basis, Obama loses by 2.6 million votes, a 9 million vote margin switch from the True Vote.

For 2012, consider the following base case scenario:
- Obama's 58% True Vote share is the basis for returning voters.
- 90% of 2008 Obama and 97% of McCain voters turn out.
- Obama wins 85% of his 2008 voters and 10% of McCain.
- Third-party (Other) and New (DNV) voters split 50/50.

Based on these assumptions, Obama wins by 6.4 million votes with a 52.4% True Vote share. There are nine vote share scenarios:

In the worst case, Obama wins 80% of returning Obama voters and 5% of returning McCain voters and loses by 5 million votes with a 48.1% share.

In the most likely base case, Obama has 85% of Obama and 10% of McCain voters and wins by 6.4 million with a 52.4% share.

In the best case, Obama has 90% of returning Obama voters and 15% of returning McCain voters and wins by 17.7 million with a 56.6% share.

Nine voter turnout scenarios
Assume Obama wins 85% of returning Obama voters and 10% of McCain voters.

In the worst case, 85% of Obama and 100% of McCain voters turn out: Obama wins by 2.6 million with a 51.0% share.

In the most likely base case, 90% of Obama and 97% of McCain voters turn out. Obama wins by 6.4 million with a 52.4% share.

In the best case, 95% of Obama and 92% of McCain voters turn out: Obama wins by 10.9 million with a 54.0% share.

As of Oct.1, the simulation indicates that Obama wins with 52% and 325 EV. Assuming that 2008 voters return proportional to unadjusted exit poll/true vote (Obama had 58%), consider the following **True Vote Model scenarios:**

No Fraud
Equal 95% turnout of returning Obama and McCain voters
Obama wins 90% of returning Obama voters and 7% of McCain
Obama wins the election with 55.3% and 380 EV.

Fraud Scenario 1
Equal 95% turnout rate of Obama and McCain voters
Obama wins 79% of returning Obama voters and 7% of McCain
(net 14% Obama defection to Romney)
Romney wins with 50.4% and 280 EV.

Fraud Scenario 2
Obama voter 62% turnout; McCain voter 95% turnout
Obama wins 90% of returning Obama, 7% of returning McCain
Romney wins with 50.1% and 275 EV.

The following True Vote sensitivity analysis never appears in the mainstream media or is mentioned by pollsters and election forecasting bloggers.

Obama is leading in the polls, but the race is "tightening". Once again, we have another media-induced "horserace".

The True Vote analysis does not consider pre-election polls. It is concerned with returning voter turnout and defection scenarios and uses the True Vote Model component.

The model shows that in order for Romney to win, he needs a 5% net turnout margin of returning McCain voters compared to Obama voters. He needs to capture nearly one out of five returning Obama voters (18% defection rate) while Obama wins just one in twenty returning McCain voters.

Obama won the 2008 state unadjusted exit poll aggregate by 58-40%. The True Vote Model indicated that he had 58%. He won the National Exit Poll by a 61-37% margin.

Given these facts assume the following:
1. Obama had 58% in 2008, not the recorded 53%.
2. New voters will split 50/50 for Obama and Romney.

The even split in new voters is a conservative assumption. Obama had 72% of new voters. Democrats have won new voters in every election since 1988.

Scenario I: Equal returning Obama and McCain 95% voter turnout and zero net defection of Obama and McCain voters. Obama has 95% of returning Obama 2008 voters and 5% of McCain voters.

Obama has 57.1% with 413 electoral votes.

Scenario II: 90% of Obama 2008 voters turn out in 2012 and 95% of McCain voters turn out. As in Scenario I, there is zero net defection of returning voters.

Obama has 55.9% with 388 electoral votes.

Scenario III: 90% of Obama voters turn out, but he only wins 90% of them. Romney still wins 95% of returning McCain voters and has a 5% turnout and defection rate advantage.

Obama has 53.5% with 334 electoral votes.

Scenario IV: Romney needs nearly one in five Obama voters. He needs a 5% turnout advantage and a 13% net defection advantage

Romney wins with 50.4% and 280 expected electoral votes.

Obama would do better than the above scenarios if he wins a majority of new voters. Republican governors have limited new Democratic registrations, cut back on early voting and imposed strict voter ID requirements. But disenfranchising voters won't be enough for Romney to win.

He needs to red-shift the votes.

CHAPTER 10

The Oregon Trail

When one admits that nothing is certain, one must, I think, admit that some things are more nearly certain than others - Bertrand Russell

A statistical analysis of Oregon's voting since 1998 when it installed a 100% paper ballot system (mail-in or hand-delivered) indicates that early voting has been a success. Recorded vote shares have closely matched telephone pre-election and exit polls in the last three presidential elections.

In 2000, Al Gore had a 47.5-47.0% margin in Oregon, a close match to the national recorded vote (Gore 48.4-Bush 47.9). Nader had 6% in Oregon and 3% nationwide. Allocating Nader vote, Gore would have won Oregon by approximately 50-47.5%. He had 50.8% in the unadjusted state exit poll national aggregate. The close match indicates that Oregon approximated the National True Vote.

In 2004, Bush improved on his 2000 recorded vote share in the battleground states and in solidly Democratic New York. But Oregon went against the grain; it shifted from Gore to Kerry. Kerry's Oregon margin was 3.7% higher than Gore. This was primarily due to Kerry's 65-13% margin in returning Nader voters and 57-41% edge in new voters.

After adjusting for undecided voters, pre-election National, Oregon and battleground polls projected that Kerry would win by 51-48%. He won the exit polls by 4%.

Mail–in voting results in high voter turnout. Kerry led by 50-44% in the final poll. After the undecided voter allocation (UVA), he was projected to win by 53-45%, matching the True Vote Model and within 1.6% of his recorded share.

The True Vote Model indicates that Kerry won by 53.5-45.5% (nearly 10 million votes). It assumed an equal 98% turnout of returning Gore and Bush voters, with 8% of Gore voters and 10%

of Bush voters defected to Kerry.

Kerry had a 51.3-47.4% margin in Oregon, compared to Bush's 50.7-48.3% recorded national share. Kerry's share was close to his 52% share in the pre-election poll and the unadjusted state exit poll aggregate (51.0-47.6%). Once again, the close match between Kerry's recorded Oregon share and the aggregate of the state exit polls indicated that Oregon reflected the True National Vote.

To believe that Oregon's mail-in/early voting system miscounted votes, one must also believe that Bush legitimately won the battleground states and therefore the national and state exit polls showed Kerry winning were wrong.

But what if the exit polls were correct? What if the votes were miscounted?   In that case, one would have to conclude that Oregon's system worked and that the votes were miscounted in the other battleground states.

In 2008, Obama led in the final Oregon pre-election poll by 56-39% and had 58.4% in the post-election telephone survey. Obama won the recorded vote by 56.7-40.4% and the True Vote Model by 56.0-42.8%. His Oregon share closely matched the 58% National True Vote and the unadjusted state exit poll aggregate. But Obama had just a 52.9% recorded national share. We can conclude that Oregon's votes were counted accurately – unlike most of the other states.

In the 2010 Midterms, Oregon's Democratic senator Ron Wyden won re-election with 57%, exactly matching the pre-election polls and Obama's share. But popular progressive Democrats in other states such as WI, IL and PA were all defeated. Their recorded vote shares were far below Obama, who won each state in a landslide.

How come Wyden won handily but other progressives in WI, PA, and IL lost? Was it due to Oregon's early voting and mandated hand recounts? Let's review Oregon's 1988-2008 presidential elections.

In 1988 Bush was the de-facto incumbent as Vice President. Dukakis led by 55.0-42.9% in the Oregon exit poll but won the recorded vote by just 51.3-46.6%. He won the unadjusted state exit poll national aggregate by 50.0-49.0%. But Bush won the national recorded vote by 53.4-45.6%.

In 1992 Bush was the incumbent. Clinton led Bush by 49.3-25.7% in the Oregon exit poll but won the state recorded vote by just 42.5-32.5%. He led the unadjusted state exit poll national aggregate by 45.7-34.8%. He won the national recorded vote by 43.0-37.4%.

In 1996, Clinton led Dole by 48.4-37.9% in the Oregon exit poll and won the state by nearly the same margin: 47.2-39.1%. He led the unadjusted state exit poll aggregate by 50.2-39.8% and won the national recorded vote in a near match: 49.2-40.7%. His 54.7% two-party Oregon share exactly matched the National recorded share.

In 2000, Gore won Oregon by 47.0-46.5% (Nader had 6.5%) and led the unadjusted state exit poll national aggregate by 50.8-44.5%. Gore won nationally by nearly the same margin (48.4-47.9%) and had a 48.3% Battleground share. The National True Vote Model indicates that he won by 49-47%.

In 2004, Bush was the incumbent. Kerry led the state pre-election polls by 48-47% and was projected to win by 51-48%. He led the Oregon pre-election poll by 50-44% and was projected to win by 53.7-45.3%.

Kerry won Oregon by 51.3-47.2%, a 3.6% improvement in margin over Gore. He won the unadjusted state exit poll aggregate by 51.1-47.0% but lost to Bush by 50.7-48.3%. Kerry had a 53.6% national share in the True Vote Model – a 10 million vote margin.

In 2008, Obama won the national recorded vote by just 52.9-45.6%, a 9.5 million vote margin. McCain was the de-facto incumbent. Obama led by 56-39% in the Oregon pre-election poll and won by 56.7-40.4%. He had 58.4% in the post-election survey, 58% in the unadjusted state exit polls and a 58% True Vote share.

The triple match is powerful confirming evidence that the vote-by-mail system worked.

National, Oregon and Battleground pre-election projections and post-election exit poll shares closely match. One must conclude that the election was stolen in the Battleground states and that Oregon's vote-by-mail system is virtually fraud-proof.

Given 2000 and 2004 votes recorded and cast, the 2004 True Vote calculation assumes:

1. Kerry and Gore had 75% of the uncounted votes
2. Annual 1.25% voter mortality
3. Equal returning Gore and Bush voter turnout rates in 2004.
4. Equal Gore and Bush returning voter defection rates.
5. Kerry won returning Nader voters by 65-13% (NEP).
6. Kerry won new voters by 59-39% nationally.

The simplifying assumption is that there was zero net defection of returning Gore and Bush voters (they cancelled each other). But the 12:22am National Exit Poll of 13,047 respondents indicates that 10% of Bush voters defected to Kerry and only 8% of Gore voters defected to Bush. The True Vote analysis shows that Kerry had a 53.7% national share assuming a net 2% defection and 53.3% assuming zero net defection. See the Recursive True Vote Model.

Two groups of three tables display the effect of various model input assumptions on Kerry's vote share. The margin of error is less than 1.5%.

Three tables display Kerry's National, Oregon and Battleground True Vote shares over a 54-63% range of new voters and 61-69% of returning Nader/other voters. Kerry wins all worst case scenarios (54% of new voters and 61% of returning Nader voters).

Gore won New York by 60.2-35.2%. Although returning Nader and new voters broke heavily for Kerry, his recorded vote-count margin declined to 58.4-40.1%. That is not plausible. Kerry led by 62-36% in the unadjusted exit poll. That is plausible.

Gore won California by 53.4-41.6%. Although returning Nader and new voters broke heavily for Kerry, his recorded vote-count margin declined to 54.3-44.1%. That is not plausible. Kerry led by 60.1-38.6% in the exit poll. That is plausible.

Why did Kerry's margin increase in Oregon, a battleground state, and decline in strongly Democratic California and New York?

Why was the exit poll so far off in California, where 29% voted on touch screens, 66% on optical scanners and 4% on punch cards?

Why was the exit poll so far off in New York, which voted exclusively on levers?

Why were the exit polls so far off in the Battleground states which voted on punched cards, levers, optical scanners and touch screens?

Final state pre-election polls were virtually all Likely Voter (LV) subsets of the full Registered Voter (RV) samples. Likely Voter subsets largely exclude "new" voters: first-timers and others who did not vote in the prior election. The Democrats won 'new voters' by an average 14% margin before Obama's whopping 44%.

By virtue of its vote by mail system, Oregon's pre-election RV polls undermine the media's objective of fooling voters into believing bogus vote counts.

Before Mail-In Ballots

1988 – Bush was Vice President.
Dukakis had 51.3% in Oregon and 45.7% National.
He did 3.2% better in the OR exit poll.

1992 – Bush was President.
Clinton had 42.5% in Oregon and 43.0% National.
He did 5.1% better in the OR exit poll.

1996 – Clinton was President.

He had 47.2% in Oregon and 49.2% National.
He did 2.2% better in the OR exit poll.

After Mail-In Ballots

2000 – Clinton was President.
Gore had 47.0% in Oregon and 48.4% National.

2004 – Bush was President.
Kerry had 51.3% in Oregon and 48.3% National.

2008 – Bush was President.
Obama had 58.4% in Oregon and 52.9% National.

Is it just a coincidence that when Clinton was the incumbent, there was just a 1.7% deviation between the Oregon and National vote shares? Is it just a coincidence that when Bush was the incumbent, there was a 3.5% deviation between the Oregon and National vote shares?

If the True Vote Model is correct and Oregon reflects the national electorate, then what does that tell us about the electoral system?

Since Oregon switched to mail-in ballots in 1998, there has been a noticeable decline in the volatility of changes in county vote shares from election to election. Before the switch to mail, there was a 0.93 correlation between 1996 and 2000 county vote share and a 5.0% standard deviation.

After the switch, there was a near-perfect 0.98 correlation between 2000 and 2004 county vote shares and a lower 2.2% standard deviation in percentage vote change. There was an even stronger 0.99 correlation for 2004 and 2008 with a very low 1.5% standard deviation in percentage vote change. The system is getting better and better.

The statistical analysis makes intuitive sense. Since the battleground states closely mirror the national electorate by definition, Oregon's recorded vote share should have been close to the other battleground states. But it was the only one that deviated sharply to Kerry.

Oregon's voting system is transparent. Optically scanned machine counts are verified by random hand-counts. Washington has also recently implemented a mail-in system.

Touch screen voting machine precincts avoid paper ballots; votes can be switched locally or at the invisible central tabulators. Optical scanners are a step in the right direction, but the system is ripe for fraud without a system similar to Oregon's mandated random hand-count of selected precincts.

Punch card machines can be rigged to void votes by double and triple-punching the ballots after the polls close – as occurred in Florida 2000. Corrupt election officials are quick to blame "stupid" voters for not properly filling out h the ballots.

Lever machines in NY, CT and PA did not use paper ballots; too few machines are placed in heavily Democratic precincts; defective machines that break down cause voters to leave the precinct; levers were "stuck" for Bush in 2004; lever gears can be shaved.

Most important, tabulation of the votes is done on computers. In NY, Gore, Kerry and Obama each enjoyed a 7% higher late (paper ballot) vote share than they did on Election Day levers. What does that tell us?

Here is an amazing statistic that very few are even aware of: Obama had 52% of the 121 million votes recorded on Election Day but he had a whopping 59% of the 10 million (paper ballot) votes recorded after Election Day. What are the odds of the 14% discrepancy? It's like a 10 million sample-size exit poll.

Kerry won new voters by 59-39% and returning Nader voters by 65-13%. In order to believe the recorded vote, you must also believe that returning Gore voters defected to Bush at a much higher rate than Bush voters to Kerry. But according to the 12:22am National Exit Poll, 10% of Bush and 8% of Gore voters defected.

The comprehensive statistical analysis indicates that Oregon's mail-in system has worked.

Sarcasm on: It would be greatly appreciated if interested readers can find a flaw in the assumptions, logic or the math and can provide contrary statistical and/or anecdotal evidence to Oregon's election officials. If compelling, they may decide to scrap vote by mail and convert to HAVA-compliant DREs, Optical scanners, Punch cards or Lever machines. Sarcasm off.

Those opposed to 100% paper ballot voting by mail or hand-delivery cite advantages in precinct voting. These include a) voters meeting friends and making new ones, b) taking time off from work to vote, c) projecting a patriotic image by voting in full view, d) looking smart by touching the computer screen, e) exercising their legs while waiting to vote and f) getting free coffee.

Voting Early on Paper Ballots vs. Election Day machines

This 2008 analysis compares exit poll discrepancies in states that voted early by mail or hand-delivered paper ballots. Approximately 30% of the 131 million total votes were cast early.

The exit poll red-shift to the GOP is negatively (-0.50) correlated to early mail or in-person voting (paper ballot). In other words, the unadjusted exit polls are a closer match to the recorded vote in early-voting states where, presumably, election fraud is minimal.

In general, exit poll discrepancies from the recorded vote (red-shift) are lower in states with a high percentage of early paper ballot voting. Conversely, states that utilize unverifiable DREs on Election Day have much higher exit poll discrepancies - as one would intuitively expect. The 15 states with the highest early voting turnout had an average 2.3% red-shift. The 15 with the lowest early turnout had an average 6.8% red-shift.

For example, the states with the highest percentage of early/hand-delivered paper ballots had the lowest red-shift: Oregon had 100% early voting and a 1.75% red-shift. Washington had 89% and 0.54%. Colorado had 79% and -1.8%.

Approximately 30% of votes cast were mailed or hand-delivered and 7% of paper ballots were recorded late (absentee, provisional, etc.). The remaining 63% that were recorded on Election Day were a combination of DREs, Optical scanners and punch card machines. Since 30% of total votes cast in 2008 were on unverifiable DREs, then about 50% of Election Day voting was on DREs. And that explains why exit poll discrepancies were highest in states that only had Election Day voting.

Now what about the votes recorded after Election Day - the Late (paper ballot) votes? How did the Democratic late vote share compare to the overall recorded vote? Not surprisingly, since late votes were cast on paper ballots (provisional, absentee, etc.), the Democrats did much better. In 2008, there were 121 million votes recorded before or on Election Day. Obama had 52.4%. But he had 59.2% of 10 million late recorded votes.

Here is the takeaway: If you have the option, vote early using paper ballots. Don't wait until Election Day to vote in cyberspace. And lobby election officials to mandate that, at minimum, the paper ballots are hand counted in randomly selected precincts or counties.

Election activists who are opposed to voting early by mail or hand-delivered paper ballots should check out Oregon, Washington and Colorado. Oregon installed its vote-by-mail system in 1998 with mandated hand-count of randomly selected counties and other safeguards.

Since 2000, Oregon has by far the best record of all the battleground states based on various statistical measures of accuracy. Washington and Colorado have recently followed suit. Is it just coincidental that the three states with the highest early voting rates had the lowest exit poll discrepancies?

If you believe that the 2004 exit polls were wrong, then you must believe that...

1- Bush won a fair election.
2- Electronic and mechanical machines accurately counted votes.
3- There was little or no fraud. Election reform is meaningless.
4- Oregon's voting was rigged since Kerry did better than Gore.
5- Pre-election polls that projected Kerry would win were wrong.
6- State and national exit polls showing a Kerry win were wrong.
7- The Oregon Kerry 52% projected share was wrong.
8- Returning Nader voters defected to Bush.
9- Bush won a majority of new voters.
10- Gore voters defected at a higher rate than Bush voters.
11- Oregon votes were padded for Kerry and Obama.
12- Voting machines in FL, OH, and NY were not tampered with.
13- Vote by mail eliminates exit polls which are wrong anyway.
14- The True Vote Model is flawed since it matched the exit polls.
15- Forcing exit polls to match the recorded vote makes sense.
16- National exit poll returning Bush voter estimate was plausible.
17- Early voting states low exit poll discrepancies were a fluke.

CHAPTER 11

Technology and Fair Elections

You can fool all of the people some of the time and some of the people all of the time, but you cannot fool all the people all of the time - Abraham Lincoln

Posters who claim that technology can never guarantee that our elections will be honest are missing the overall by focusing on only one factor in the equation. They claim that any system can be hacked (which is true) – but they leave it at that. They fail to consider that technology, used in conjunction with low-tech hand-counts, provides a more secure voting system than hand-counts alone.

Current voting systems are designed to be hacked. We need systems that are designed to work. It's that simple. Data redundancy, auditable processes, open source code, non-proprietary systems, expert design (not r/w hacks); voters can confirm their own vote. What's wrong with that?

Let experts check the code and agree that it would work. As the computer security expert Steve Spoonamore has indicated, you just need to make sure that votes are added. There should not be code to subtract. It's not rocket science. If voters have the ability to check their vote after it has been transmitted to a tabulator and find a mistake, they can report it. It is a citizen auditable process. It's just common sense.

Spoonamore has analyzed Diebold ATM software, but is prohibited from looking at Diebold's voting machine code. He says that each voter should be allowed to check their vote electronically. He wants a system of "freeware", like Open Source.

What he doesn't mention is the additional benefit in that election officials cannot be coerced to install systems that consistently fail inspection procedures.

Voters should own the hardware and the software. They should be able to check that their votes were counted as cast. We should have the best of both worlds: A hybrid system of hand-counted ballot summaries posted at the precinct as well as online. Each ballot contains an anonymous voter code. It's a self-auditing system.

The key is data redundancy and transparency. An Open Source/Internet system can provide a solution. The Diebold and ES&S voting machines and central tabulators use proprietary code for one reason: they are designed to be manipulated. Non-proprietary hardware and Open Source software is the solution, not the current systems from right-wing corporations that steal elections while Congress looks the other way.

The solution is simple, so simple that it has never been and will never be proposed by corrupt politicians and election officials. The use of current closed systems by election officials and their refusal to consider an Open Source solution is itself proof that it would work. Virtually all voters would have online access to their vote. And many would check to see that it was correct. They would in effect be the auditors and the exit pollsters.

To the skeptics, a True Vote can be achieved only by hand-counting the ballots at the voting site (they neglect to mention the need to tabulate all other precincts).

To the technologists, a True Vote can be best achieved hand-counting ballots, posted results at the voting site and providing a voter-verified tabulation of all precincts online.

The skeptics offer no solution, just the mantra that technology is incapable of insuring fair elections because every system can be hacked. They fail to consider the primary goal of any security system: data redundancy and built-in safeguards to detect fraud. They speak with a tone of final authority. How do they know a nearly foolproof system cannot be developed?

Computer experts want fair elections. Why not create a prototype? Refusal to even consider a technical solution makes no sense. What if the experts could provide such a hybrid solution? Would the naysayers accept it?

The skeptics display an arrogance of supreme authority. They claim that technology would never work and that corrupt election officials can always outsmart experts in computer security and software design of non-proprietary, robust hardware/software based election systems. But how do they know that? The fault lies not in our technology, but in the failure to even consider a prototype.

One skeptic claimed that those who believed that technology would work *"refuse to see that transparency, simplicity, comprehension and control of the electoral process by the citizen-voters is essential to their opponents' view of what is required for democratic process, and that no technologically sophisticated "solution" can satisfy those requirements"*.

But an Open Source system is the only one which can provide the l transparency that voters need to have confidence in, knowing that they owned the hardware and the software and could verify that their votes (and those of others) have been counted correctly.

Another claim is that voting systems are unlike other *"systems under the operational control of the institutions that maintains a stake in those systems operating properly for the benefit of those institutions, and that the electoral process by its nature is one of divided interests. (Power tends to corrupt, and absolute power corrupts absolutely.)"*

But the problem is not technology, rather those who have the power to use it and fail to do so. A voting system could be designed with in which the probability would be extremely low that corrupt election officials and hackers would be able to insert algorithms to miscount the votes or penetrate remotely.

Most election officials have limited knowledge of hardware and software.

In Wisconsin, the fraud was transparent, whether by stuffing ballot bags or stacking 50 ballots in a row in Verona for the Republican Prosser who had 33% in the municipality.

The theft would never have been possible if a robust, transparent, data redundant system was in place. In the highly unlikely event that a hacker was able to break into the online database, the totals would not match the hard copy posted at the precinct and would be noticed by voters who checked their votes online.

"I'm sure that I could design a electronic voting system that is guaranteed to work properly if I could continue to control all the actors and all the checks and balances along the way — and if I stayed honest — but so what? Why should voters want or need such a system? There is no reason for voters to trust me, and even if they did the system (not their method for "checking" how their vote was counted) would remain opaque to them, and there would be no trace of collective participatory democracy in the vote counting process, which like the so-called negativists I consider important, if not essential, to the process".

Even if he could design such a system, why would he want to do it all by himself? Why not collaborate with other experts who could check each other's work? Why not test a prototype? Even the system is "opaque", the only relevant question is: would it solve the problem? Does he really believe that voters care to know the details of how the system is designed? Do they have a clue as to how their financial transactions are processed?

Of course there is no reason to trust him; that's why he would have to work with a team of professionals in designing the system. There is no reason for voters to trust him if others cannot revue his code to make sure that 1+1 is always equal to 2 and that there is never a reduction in the vote count.

The claim there would be no trace of collective participation in the vote-counting process is false. Voters would participate in the system when it counts: by checking to make sure that votes posted on the precinct wall match the data uploaded to the Internet.

There is no way to accomplish that now. But if they had a copy of their ballot and were able to check that it was properly recorded on the Net they could do it.

"And exactly how would this stop ballot box stuffing? Ghost voters do NOT check their ballots on the internet. Counting the hard copy ballots at the precinct that the voters marked. Counting the night of the election while ballots are still in full view and custody of numerous observers — that isn't simple? Guess not".

Voters would be assigned sequential IDs that would be recorded in poll books. A summary of votes cast would be posted periodically on the precinct wall. The number of entries in the poll book would have to match the posted summary. The corresponding ballot records would be uploaded and sorted by Voter ID. The number of data records would have to match the posted summary at the precinct.

Naysayers forget that total votes cast must be tabulated for each precinct in each county. Would it be done by hand calculator or abacus or computer? How would voters know that their vote and those of others in other precincts would be tabulated correctly? Where would they go to check their vote other than on the precinct wall?

There is just one feasible location where they could check that their vote was tabulated correctly – and that is online in the comfort of their own home. Is there better alternative? Or should we just trust that the central tabulations were not rigged?

In Wisconsin, election results were not posted in full public view. How, when and by whom were the DRE poll tapes generated? Who wrote the proprietary software? Who manufactured the voting machines? We already know that: right wing organizations. Why were ballots kept in sealed bags in the Waukesha clerk's office? Why was she allowed to use unique software? Could anyone else view the code?

Could she have hacked an Open Source system developed by professionals to run on non-proprietary hardware? Could she have changed the hard copy results posted on the wall of each voting location if it was guarded by several independent monitors? Not likely.

But even if she were able to bribe the monitors, could she have a) sneaked into the home of each voter whose vote was changed on the hard copy posted at the precinct, b) find the voter's ballot copy, c) forged it to match the copy posted at the voting location, d) hacked the uploaded posted summaries and e) installed a virus on each voter's computer to prevent them from going online to check their own vote and location total?

The only way it could happen was if she were cloned into thousands of Superwomen. But miracles do happen. After all, they found 50 consecutive ballots for Prosser in Verona, a town that voted 67% for Kloppenburg.

The Election Transparency Project

The Humboldt (CA) County Election Transparency Project (ETP) is a documented case in which technology uncovered vote miscounts. Volunteers scanned ballots after the election to verify the integrity of the Diebold/Premier machines. The images were made publicly available and used TEV ballot counting software

They found that 197 ballots were deleted by the Diebold/Premier GEMS software used by Humboldt County to tally the vote. The software glitch resulted in the certification of inaccurate election results.

The Election Administration Research Center at UC Berkeley site contains ballot images that were scanned during this project (the same images can also be obtained on DVD from the Elections Office).The ballot extraction code reads the ballot image and uses OCR to automatically determine the candidates listed on the ballot. It reads the images and stores the results in a database.

The ETP is overseen by officials from the Humboldt County Elections Office. However, the "elbow grease" of this project, with a couple of exceptions, is done by volunteers who care about the integrity of elections.

The volunteers, working on weekends, holidays, and evenings, use a high-end office scanner to scan all paper ballots cast in an election. The scanner produces digital images of the ballots. The ballots are "digitally signed" to mark their authenticity and uploaded to the Internet for distribution. These images are also available on DVD at the Elections Office.

One notable feature is that each ballot is imprinted with a unique serial number before it is imaged. Part of the serial number contains information about on the box the ballot comes from. This feature "ties together" an image on the Internet with the paper ballot.

A site belonging to ETP volunteer Mitch Trachtenberg contains an Open Source software program that automates the counting of these ballot images. This auditing tool is quite valuable in producing a tally that can be used to compare against the results produced by software that is not subject to inspection by members of the general public. In short, this tool alleviates the need of counting ballots by hand and does so in a transparent manner.

CHAPTER 12

Myths and Anomalies

The history of our race, and each individual's experience, are sown thick with evidence that a truth is not hard to kill and that a lie told well is immortal - Mark Twain

"False recall" was the final argument promoted by exit poll naysayers to explain away the mathematically impossible 43/37% returning Bush/Gore voter mix in the 2004 Final National Exit Poll (NEP). It was an attempt to cast doubt on the preliminary NEP and the unadjusted state exit poll aggregate (Kerry won by 51-48%). It was a last-ditch attempt to maintain the fiction that Bush really did win fairly and that the unadjusted and preliminary exit polls "behaved badly". The bottom line: exit polls should not be trusted (or even used) here in the U.S. - but they work fine in far away places like Ukraine and Georgia.

"False recall" stated that the mathematically impossible Final NEP mix was due to returning Gore voters who had the temerity of misstating their past vote to the exit pollsters, claiming they actually voted for Bush. This strange behavior was apparently due to faulty memory – a "slow-drifting fog" unique to Gore voters and/or a desire to be associated with Bush, the official "winner" of the 2000 election. The fact that he actually lost by 540,000 recorded votes was dismissed as irrelevant.

The unadjusted 2004 NEP on the Roper website should finally put "false recall" to eternal rest. Of the 13,660 respondents, 7064 (51.7%) said they voted for Kerry, 6414 (47.0%) for Bush and 182 (1.3%) for other third-parties. The NEP is a subset of unadjusted state exit polls (76,000 respondents). The weighted average of the aggregate state polls indicated that Kerry was a 51.1-47.5% winner.

But what did the respondents really say about how they voted in 2000? Of the 3,182 respondents who were asked, 1,222 (38.4%) said they voted for Gore, 1,257 (39.5%) said Bush and 119 (3.75%) were third party votes. The remaining 585 (18.4%) were either first-timers or others who did not vote in 2000.

When the actual Bush/Gore 39.5/38.4% returning voter mix and the 12:22am preliminary NEP vote shares are used to calculate the vote shares, Kerry has 51.7% – exactly matching the unadjusted NEP. But Kerry must have done better than that. The unadjusted 2000 exit poll indicated that Gore won by 5-6 million, so there had to be more returning Gore voters than Bush voters in 2004.

Although there is no evidence that Gore voters came to love Bush (even after he stole the 2000 election), or that returning Gore voters were more forgetful and dishonest than Bush voters, the "false recall" canard has been successful in keeping the "bad exit poll" myth alive. Such is the power of the mainstream media.

"False recall" was the equivalent of the famous "Hail Mary" touchdown pass. It followed the "reluctant Bush responder" (rBr) and "Swing vs. Red-shift" arguments, both of which had been refuted (see the links below).

Since unadjusted 2004 NEP data was not provided in the mainstream media, "false recall" was a possibility, however remote and ridiculous the premise. It was a very thin reed that has been surprisingly resilient. Apparently it still is to Bill Clinton, Al Franken and even Michael Moore. Not to mention the mainstream "liberal" media who continue to maintain the fiction that Bush really did win.

We now have clear proof that in order to match the recorded vote, the exit pollsters had to adjust the NEP returning voter mix from the (already adjusted) 12:22am timeline; the 41/39% mix was changed to an impossible 43/37%. But they had to do more than just that. They had to inflate the 12:22am Bush shares of new and returning voters to implausible levels.

The earlier proof that the returning voter mix was adjusted in the Final NEP (even though it was mathematically impossible) to match the recorded vote is confirmed by the data itself. Now, with the actual responses to the question "Who did you vote for in 2000", there is no longer any question as to whether Gore voters forgot or lied or were in a slow moving fog.

The "pristine" results show that the actual Bush/Gore returning voter mix (39.5/38.4%) differs substantially from the artificial, mathematically impossible Final NEP (43/37%) mix.

This is irrefutable evidence that the Final NEP is not a true sample. Of course, we knew this all along. The exit pollsters admit it but they don't like to talk about the fact that it's standard operating procedure to force ALL final exit polls to match the recorded vote. This is easily accomplished by adjusting returning voter turnout from the previous election to get the results to "fit". Of course, the mainstream media political pundits never talk about it. So how would you know?

Political sites such as CNN, NY Times and realclearpolitics.com still display the 2004 Final National Exit poll and perpetuate the fiction that Bush won. But it's not just the 2004 election. ALL FINAL exit polls published by the mainstream media (congressional and presidential) are forced to match the recorded vote. Unadjusted exit polls don't "behave badly" – but the adjusted Finals sure do.

"False recall" followed the "reluctant Bush responder" (rBr) and "Swing vs. Red-shift" arguments (see links below), both of which have been refuted.

The Final NEP is mathematically impossible since the number of returning Bush voters implied by the 43% weighting is 52.6 million (122.3 million votes were recorded in 2004). Bush only had 50.46 million recorded votes in 2000. Approximately 2.5 million died; therefore the number of returning Bush voters must have been less than 48 million. Assuming 98% turnout, there were 47 million returning Bush voters, 5.6 million fewer than implied by the Final NEP.

Based on 12:22am NEP vote shares, Kerry wins by 10m votes with 53.2% – assuming equal 98% turnout of returning Bush and Gore voters. He wins by 7 million given 98/90% Bush/Gore turnout. Total votes cast in 2000 and 2004 are used to calculate returning and new voters.

Kerry's vote share trend was a constant 51% at the 7:33pm (11027) and 12:22am (13047) time lines. Kerry gained 1085 votes and Bush 1025 from 7:33pm to 12:22am. Third-parties declined by 90 due to the 4% to 3% change in share of the electorate.

False recall is disproved in a number of ways.
1. It is based on a 3168 subset of the Final NEP 13660 respondents who were asked how they voted in 2000. But all 13660 were asked who they JUST voted for.

2. In the preliminary 12:22am NEP of 13047 respondents, approximately 3025 of the 3168 were asked how they voted in 2000. This estimate was derived by applying the same 95.4% percentage (13047/13660) to the 3168. The weighted result indicated that returning Bush voters comprised 41% (50.1m) of the electorate.

The Final NEP "Voted in 2000" cross tab (and all other cross tabs) was forced to match the recorded vote. This required that 43% (52.6m) of the electorate had to be returning Bush voters. The increase in the returning Bush 2000 voter share of the 2004 electorate (from 41% at 12:22am to 43% in the Final) was clearly impossible since it was based on a mere 143 (25% of 613) additional respondents.

3) There was an impossible late switch in respondent totals. Between 7:33pm and 12:22am, the trend was consistent: Kerry gained 254 votes, Bush 239. Third-parties declined by 13. But between 12:22 am and the Final, Kerry's total declined by 13, Bush gained 182 and third party lost 26.

4) It was also impossible that returning Bush voters would increase from 41% to 43% (122) and returning Gore voters would decline from 39% to 37% (8). Regardless, the Final 43/37% split was mathematically impossible. It implied there were 5.6 million more returning Bush voters than could have voted, assuming that 47 (98%) of the 48 million who were alive turned out.

5) The increase in Bush's share of new voters from 41% to 45% (+31) was impossible; there were just 24 additional new voters. Kerry lost 2.

6) The changes in the Gender demographic were impossible. The Kerry trend was consistent at the 11027 and 13047 respondent time lines. Kerry gained 1085 and Bush 1025. Third-parties declined by 90.

7) There was an impossible shift to Bush among the final 613 respondents (from 13,047 to 13,660). Kerry's total declined by 99, while Bush gained 706. Third-parties gained 6. That could not have happened unless weights and vote shares were adjusted by a human. In other words, it could not have been the result of an actual sample.

8. False recall assumes that 43/37% was a sampled result. But we have just shown that it is mathematically impossible because a) it implies there were 5.6 million more returning Bush voters than could have voted in 2004 and b) the 41/39% split at 12:22am could not have changed to 43/37% in the Final with just 143 additional respondents in the "Voted 2000" category.

9. The exit pollsters claim that it is standard operating procedure to force the exit poll to match the recorded vote. The Final was forced to match the recorded vote by a) adjusting the returning Bush/Gore voter mix to an impossible 43/37% and b) simultaneously increasing the Bush shares of returning Bush, Gore and new voters to implausible levels using impossible adjustments.

10. Just reviewing the time line, it is obvious that the exit pollsters did in fact adjust weights and vote shares to force a match the recorded vote. It's Standard Operating Procedure. But it immediately invalidates the naysayer claim that the 43/37 split was due to Gore voter false recall. No, it was due to exit poll data manipulation.

11. Which is more believable: a) that the exit pollsters followed the standard procedure of forcing the poll to match the vote, or b) that at least 8% more returning Gore voters claimed they voted for Bush in 2000 than returning Bush voters claimed they voted for Gore?

12. As indicated above, there was a maximum number of returning Bush 2000 voters who could have voted in 2004: those who were still living. So the 43/37% split is not only impossible, it is also irrelevant. It doesn't matter what the returning voters said regarding their 2000 vote. We already know the four-year voter mortality rate (5%) and maximum livingvoter turnout (98%).

13. False recall assumes that the returning voter mix is a sampled result. But the 4% increase in differential between returning Bush and Gore voters (from 2% to 6%) is impossible since the total number of respondents increased by just 143 (from 3025 to 3168).

14. The false recall claim is based on NES surveys of 500-600 respondents which appear to indicate that voters misstate their past votes. **But the reported deviations are based on the prior recorded vote – not the True Vote**. There has been an average of 7 million net uncounted votes in each of the last eleven elections. The majority (70-80%) were Democratic. In 2000, there were 5.4 million.

When measured against the True Vote (based on total votes cast, reduced by mortality and voter turnout), the average deviations are near zero. Therefore, the NES respondents told the truth about their past vote.

15. The 2006 and 2008 Final National Exit Polls were forced to match the recorded vote with impossible 49/43% and 46/37% returning Bush/Kerry voter percentages. The 2008 Final required 12 million more returning Bush than Kerry voters.

These anomalies are just additional proof that false recall is totally bogus – a final "Hail Mary" pass to divert, confuse and cover-up the truth. The exit pollsters just did what they are paid to do.

Do you believe the Final 2004 National Exit Poll (13,660 respondents)? The Final NEP was forced to match the recorded vote (Bush 50.7-48.3%).

If you do, then you must also believe in miracles. The Final indicates that there were 6 million more returning Bush 2000 voters than were still living in 2004 – a 110% turnout. The pollsters had to create 6 million Bush phantoms in order to force the Final to match the recorded vote.

Logic 101: If an impossible number of returning Bush 2000 voters is required for the 2004 National Exit Poll to match the recorded vote, then the 2004 recorded vote must also be impossible. Ergo, the FINAL exit poll and the official vote count must both be fraudulent.

And if you still believe in 6 million Bush phantoms, then you must not believe:
1) the unadjusted NEP (13,660 respondents). Kerry had 51.7%.
2) the unadjusted state exit polls (76,192). Kerry had 51.1%.

Let's calculate the returning Gore and Bush percentage mix of 2004 voters, assuming 1.25% annual mortality and 97% Gore/Bush turnout of living voters.

We apply the following methods:
1) Votes cast: Gore 51.0 million recorded votes + 75% of 6 million uncounted: Gore is a winner by 50.0-47.3%.
The returning Gore/Bush share of the 2004 electorate: 41.0/38.2%.
Kerry wins by 53.2-45.4%

2) 2000 Unadjusted State Exit Poll aggregate: Gore by 50.8-45.5%.
Returning Gore/Bush share of 2004 vote: 41.4/37.0%
Kerry wins by 53.9-44.7%

3) 2000 Unadjusted National Exit Poll: Gore by 48.5-46.3%
Returning Gore/Bush share of 2004 electorate: 39.4/37.6%
Kerry wins by 52.9-45.7%

4) 2004 National Exit Poll (adjusted to matched recorded vote)
Returning Gore/Bush share: 37/43% (impossible Bush turnout)
Bush by 50.7-48.3%

Given the 2000 recorded vote, unadjusted NEP (13660 respondents) vote shares and a 98% turnout of living Bush 2000 voters, Kerry needed just a 73% turnout of Gore voters to tie Bush.

For Bush to win his 3.0 million "mandate", there had to be a 64% turnout of Gore voters. If you believe that, there is a great Chinese restaurant in lower Manhattan near a famous old bridge that is for sale. Assuming an equal 98% turnout of Gore and Bush voters, Kerry won the True Vote by more than 10 million votes with a 53.6% vote share.

2004 Myths and Anomalies

1 - Myth: The media exhaustively analyzed state and national pre-election and exit poll data and documented evidence of vote suppression and miscounts.

Fact: raw exit poll precinct data has never been made public. The pundits have failed to explain the impossible anomalies in the final national and state exit polls.

2 - Myth: There are many explanations why the exit polls were wrong in 2004.

Kerry voters sought to be interviewed; Bush voters were reluctant; young interviewers sought out Kerry voters; returning Gore voters lied to the exit pollsters and said that they voted for Bush in 2000; exit polls are not random samples; exit polls in the U.S. are not designed to catch election fraud; early exit polls overstated the Kerry vote; women voted early; Republicans voted late; Gore voters defected to Bush at twice the rate that Bush voters defected to Kerry, etc.

Fact: none are supported by the evidence. In fact, they are refuted by the exit pollsters own data and polling timeline.

3 - Myth: The votes were fairly counted.

Fact: There is no way to prove that. Voting machines are vulnerable and the code is proprietary; there is no chain of evidence or hand-recounts of paper ballots. The 2004 Vote Census indicates that 125.7 million votes were cast and just 122.3m recorded. Investigative reporter Greg Palast provided government data which confirmed the Census: at least 3 million ballots were never counted.

4 - Myth: Democrats failed to attract first-time voters.

Fact: According to the National Exit Poll (NEP), the Democratic candidates won first-time voters by solid margin in every election since 1992. In 2008 Obama won new voters by 71-27%. The 2004 NEP timeline indicated that Kerry had 62% of new voters at 4pm, 59% at 9pm and 57% at 1222am. But the Final NEP was forced to match the recorded vote. It indicated that Kerry had just 54% of new voters, a massive 8% decline from the earlier share.

5 - Myth: Bush's 48% Election Day approval rating was not a major factor.

Fact: Since 1976 all presidential incumbents with less than 50% approval lost re-election (Ford, Carter, Bush 1). Incumbents above 50% won (Eisenhower, Johnson, Nixon, Reagan, and Clinton). There was a near-perfect 0.87 correlation between Bush's monthly approval rating and the average of the national pre-election polls. The correlation was confirmed when Kerry won the National Exit Poll by 51-48%.

6 - Myth: Bush gained 9% over 2000 in heavily Democratic urban locations.

Fact: That Urban Legend is counter-intuitive: Bush lost 3% in highly Republican small towns and rural areas. He stole millions of votes in urban and suburban locations.

7 - Myth: Bush voters voted late on Election Day.

Fact: Kerry led by a constant 51-48% in the National Exit Poll timeline from 8349 to the final 13660 respondents.

8 - Myth: The final pre-election polls did not match the exit polls.

Fact: After undecided voters were allocated, the weighted pre-election state (Kerry 47.9-Bush 46.9%) and national polls (Kerry 47.2-46.9%) closely matched the aggregate weighted unadjusted state (51.7-47.0%) and national exit polls (51.1-47.9%).

9 - Myth: Bogus assumptions were used in the pre-election Election Model which forecast that Kerry would win 337 electoral votes.

Fact: The only (conservative) assumption was that Kerry would capture at least 75% of the undecided vote. Popular and electoral vote projections were confirmed by the 2004 Election Simulation and True Vote Model.

10 - Myth: There is no evidence that undecided voters break for the challenger.

Fact: Historical evidence shows that undecided voters break for the challenger at least 80% of the time – especially when the incumbent is unpopular. Bush had a 48% average approval rating. World-class pollsters Harris and Zogby reported that late polling indicated Kerry would win 60-80% of the undecided vote. Gallup allocated 88% of undecided voters to Kerry.

11 - Myth: Bush was leading in the final pre-election polls.

Fact: Kerry led Bush by 1% in the weighted state polls and tied at 47% based on the national 18-poll average. After allocating the 5% of voters who were undecided, Kerry was a 51-48% winner.

12 - Myth: Non-response exit poll bias (reluctant Bush responder) was the reason 43 states red-shifted from the exit polls to the recorded vote to Bush.

Fact: Response rates were highest in Bush strongholds.

13 - Myth: It was just a fluke that Oregon was the only battleground state where Kerry did better than Gore.

Fact: Oregon is the only state which votes by mail or hand-delivered paper ballots and also mandates hand counts of randomly selected counties – a powerful election fraud deterrent. Kerry did worse than Gore in the other battleground states because none of them had an equivalent fraud deterrent. DRE touch screen computers that were used to calculate 30% of the votes are unverifiable. Optical scanned paper ballots were not hand-counted.

14 - Myth: 2004 exit polls did not indicate that electronic voting machines are fraudulent.

Fact: All voting methods had high discrepancies – except for paper ballots which had just a 2% average discrepancy. Lever machine precincts had the highest (11%) discrepancies. Unverifiable touch screen (DRE) and optical scan precincts each had 7%. Of 88 reported touch screen vote switching incidents, 86 were from Kerry to Bush (a zero probability).

15 - Myth: The exit polls behaved "badly".

Fact: Final state and national exit polls are always forced to match the recorded vote. It's standard operating procedure. But the media pundits assume a fraud-free election. Millions of uncounted votes prove that elections have been anything but fraud-free. And the 6 million phantom Bush voters required by the Final 2004 National Exit Poll to match the recorded vote prove that it cannot be correct.

16 - Myth: Kerry led in the early exit polls, but Bush passed him in the final.

Fact 1: Kerry led the National Exit Poll (NEP) by a constant 51-48% from start to end. He led at 4pm (8349 respondents), 730pm (11027) and 1222am (13047).

Kerry led the state aggregate unadjusted state exit polls by 51.1-47.9%. He won the unadjusted NEP (13660) by 51.7-47.0), but Bush won the adjusted Final NEP (13660) by 51-48%. The Final was forced to match the recorded vote.

Fact 2: It is a mathematical impossibility that 613 additional exit poll respondents could cause Kerry's 51-48% margin (at 12:22am after the polls closed) to flip to Bush. And they didn't. Kerry led the unadjusted 13660 by the 51-48%. But the Final NEP (13660) was forced to match the recorded vote by switching respondents from Kerry to Bush.

17 - Myth: The exit poll margin of error was too low.

Fact: Even assuming a 60% "cluster effect", the probabilities were near zero. The exit poll discrepancies exceeded the MoE in 29 states for Bush and just one for Kerry – a zero probability. Assuming a 30% cluster effect, the MoE was exceeded in 24 states for Bush.

18 - Myth: There is nothing suspicious about the fact that all 21 Eastern Time Zone states red-shifted from the exit poll in favor of Bush.

Fact: The probability of the one-sided red shift is equivalent to coin-flipping 21 consecutive heads: 1 in 2 million. But 14 exit polls deviated beyond the margin of error – a ZERO probability.

19 - Myth: Exit polls are not true random samples.

Fact: Exit pollsters Edison-Mitofsky state in the notes to the National Exit Poll and Methods Statement that respondents were randomly-selected with an overall 1% margin of error for 10,000 respondents. But there were over 13,000 respondents. The MoE was 1.1% after adding a 30% "cluster effect".

20 - Myth: Bush voters were reluctant to respond to exit pollsters.

Fact: This is contradicted by the Final National Exit Poll. The Final indicated that returning Bush 2000 voters comprised 43% of the 2004 electorate compared to just 37% for Gore voters (i.e. there were 7 million more returning Bush than Gore voters). But Gore won the unadjusted exit poll by 50-45% (3-6 million votes). The rBr canard was also contradicted by a linear regression analysis. Non-response rates were highest in Kerry strongholds, indicating that most non-responders were in fact Kerry voters.

21 - Myth: Ohio, Florida and National exit polls show that Bush won.

Fact: FINAL State and National exit polls are ALWAYS adjusted (forced) to match the recorded vote even when the votes are miscounted – as they were in 2004. Unadjusted state and national exit polls showed Kerry winning by 54-46% in Ohio, and 51-48% in Florida and National.

22 - Myth: The Final NEP 43/37 Bush/Gore returning voter mix is possible.

Fact: the 43/37 mix was not a polling result; it was contrived to force a match to the recorded vote. This is the incontrovertible proof: Kerry had 7074 (51.71%) of the unadjusted 13660 NEP respondents. Bush had 6414 (46.95%). Of the 13660, 3182 were asked who they voted for in 2000: 1257 (39.50%) said Bush, 1221 (38.37%) said Gore.

If the 39.5/38.37 mix is applied to the 12:22am NEP vote shares, Kerry has 51.74%, exactly matching the unadjusted NEP. This exposes the 43/37 returning voter mix. It additional proofs that the NEP was forced to match the recorded vote-not an actual sample.

The mix could not have from changed from 41/39 at 12:22am to 43/37 with just 613 additional respondents. Bush 2000 voters could not have comprised 43% (52.6 million) of the 122.3 million votes recorded in 2004 since he only had 50.5 million votes in 2000. Approximately 2.5 million Bush 2000 voters died prior to the 2004 election. Therefore, there were at most 48.0 million returning Bush voters in 2004 – assuming an impossible 100% turnout.

If 98% turned out, there were 47.0 million returning Bush voters. Therefore, there had to be 5.6 million (52.6 less 47.0) phantom voters.

23 - Myth: The Democratic Underground "Game" thread showed that Bush could have won with a feasible and plausible 39/39% returning Bush/Gore mix.

Fact: In order to force a match to the recorded vote, the NEP vote shares also had to be adjusted to implausible levels far beyond the margin of error. The scenario required a) Kerry's share of new voters reduced from 57% to 52.9%, b) Bush's share of Gore voters increased from 8% to 14.6% and c) Bush 2000 returning voter defection rate reduced from 10% to 7.2%.

24 - Myth: The near-zero correlation between vote swing from 2000 to 2004 and exit poll red-shift "kills the fraud argument".

Fact: "Swing vs. Red-shift" was based on an invalid premise and twisted logic. It uses the 2000 and 2004 recorded votes to prove there was no fraud in 2004. But the votes were obviously fraudulent (there were 6 million uncounted votes in 2000 and 4 million in 2004). There is a strong correlation between vote swing and red-shift when unadjusted state exit polls are used as proxies for the True Vote.

25 - Myth: "False Recall" explains the NEP 43/37 Bush/Gore returning voter mix.

Fact: Of the 13660 NEP respondents, 7064 (51.7%) voted for Kerry and 6414 (46.9%) for Bush. Only 3182 were asked who they voted for in 2000: 1257 (39.5%) said Bush, 1221 (38.4%) said Gore. Using the 39.5/38.4% mix and 12:22am NEP vote shares, Kerry wins by 51.8-46.8%, exactly matching the unadjusted NEP, putting the lie to the published Final NEP (Bush 50.7-48.3%).

The Final was derived by forcing a match based on a fictitious 43/37 returning Bush/Gore mix. The unadjusted 13660 sample had to be "adjusted" to have the Final NEP match the fraudulent recorded share. Bottom line: the rationale for the 43/37% returning voter mix is no longer debatable. It was clearly a forced fictional result and not an actual sample.

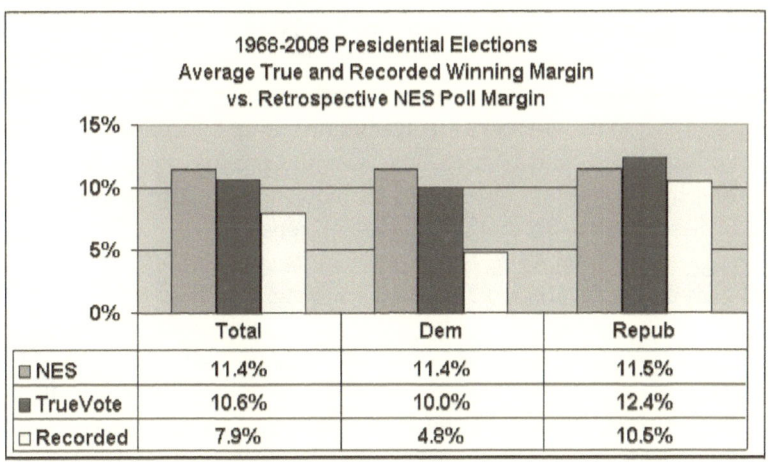

	Total	Dem	Repub
■ NES	11.4%	11.4%	11.5%
■ TrueVote	10.6%	10.0%	12.4%
□ Recorded	7.9%	4.8%	10.5%

26 - Myth: A "slow drifting fog" caused Gore voters to say they voted for Bush.

Fact: NES used 2000 and 2004 (105.4m and 122.3m) recorded votes as a baseline for the survey, rather than True Votes cast (110.8m and 125.7m). There were nearly 6 million uncounted votes in 2000, of which approximately 4.5 million were for Gore. Counting these votes, Gore won the True Vote by 2-3 million – not the 540,000 recorded. And similarly Kerry won 3 of 4 million uncounted votes. Using votes cast as the baseline shows that NES respondents did not misstate their 2000 vote.

Fact: Only 3182 (23%) of 13660 of respondents were asked how they voted in 2000. The other 10,478 were asked who they just voted for in 2004. Voters do not forget who they voted for in the previous election, much less how they just voted a few minutes before.

False recall was obviously not a factor in the pre-election polls which matched the exit polls after undecided voters were allocated. And now that the unadjusted National Exit Poll data has been released, we know that exactly 51.7% of the respondents voted for Kerry – and just 47.0% for Bush.

27 - Myth: Returning Gore voters misrepresented their 2000 vote to the exit pollsters because they wanted to be associated with Bush.

Fact: Bush had a 48% approval rating on Election Day. The majority of new voters were Democrats and Independents who gave Bush 10-20% approval. Gore was the popular vote winner in 2000 – by 2-3 million True Votes. So why would Gore voters want to be associated with Bush? It makes no sense.

28 - Myth: Bush gained 12 million new voters in 2004.

Fact: Simple arithmetic shows that Bush needed more than 16 million new voters. He had 50.5m recorded votes in 2000. Approximately 2.5m died and 1.0m did not return to vote in 2004.

Therefore, 47 million Bush 2000 voters returned to vote in 2004. He needed 15 million (68%) of 22 million new voters to get his recorded 62 million.

But according to the 12:22am National Exit Poll, he had just 41% (9 million) of new voters, a full 7 million (27%) fewer than he needed. The probability that 68% of new voters were for Bush is absolute zero.

29 - Myth: Bush won by a 3 million vote "mandate".

Fact: Gore won by 540,000 recorded votes so Kerry had a head-start. At the 12:22am National Exit Poll timeline, Kerry had 57% of new voters (first-timers and others who did not vote in 2000). He won returning Nader voters by 64-17% and 10% of Bush voters.

Just 8% of Gore voters defected to Bush. So how could Bush have won? He needed a massive net defection of Gore voters.

And Gore won by 3-6 million votes – not the 540,000 recorded. The Bush "win" was clearly impossible.

30 - Myth: Sensitivity analysis does not prove anything.

Fact: It is proof beyond a reasonable doubt since Kerry's worst case (implausible) scenario win probability was greater than 90% and the base case (plausible) scenario was greater than 99%.

31 - Myth: Bush's share of females (48%) increased by 4.2% over his 2000 share.

Fact: That's implausible since his share of males declined by 0.2%. It is totally counter-intuitive that females would defect to Bush and males would defect to Kerry. In the 12:22am NEP, females voted 54-45% for Kerry.

32 - Myth: Bush won Ohio.

Fact: There is much documented evidence of uncounted and switched votes, besides massive voter disenfranchisement. Two election workers were convicted of rigging the recount. Fifty-six of 88 county voting records were destroyed.

The final Zogby poll had Kerry leading by 50-47%. Kerry led the unadjusted Ohio exit poll by 54.1-45.9% (10.9% WPD). Kerry led the adjusted 12:40am Composite by 52.1-47.9%.

33 - Myth: Bush won Florida by 52-47%, a 368,000 vote margin.

Fact: Democrats had a 41-37% registration advantage in Touch Screen counties and a 42-39% advantage in Optical Scan) counties. Kerry won DRE counties (3.86 million votes) by 51-47%. Bush won OS counties (3.43 million) by an implausible 57-42%.

Kerry won the exit poll by 50.9-48.3%. In 2000, Gore had 70% of 180,000 uncounted, spoiled votes, so he won the state by at least 50,000 votes. A Dan Rather special on voting machines proved that poor-quality paper used by punch card machines was a major cause of ballot spoilage in heavily Democratic precincts.

34 - Myth: NY pre-election and final exit polls (Kerry 58.5-40.2%) were correct. The unadjusted exit poll Kerry (64.1-34.4%) was wrong.

Fact: New York and California were rigged to inflate Bush's popular vote margin and provided 2.0 million of his 3.0 million vote "mandate".

NY voted 60.5% for Gore, 35.4% for Bush and 4.1% for Nader. This is just one example of the impossible scenarios required to match the 2004 NY vote. Bush needed
a) 100% of Nader voters (he had 17% nationally)
b) 50% of new voters (he had 41% nationally)
c) 11% of returning Gore voters (he had 8% nationally)

The clincher: Kerry's NY share was 10% higher than his national share. How could Bush have done so much better in heavily Democratic NY with returning Gore, Nader and new voters than he did nationally? It is counter-intuitive and makes no sense.

Pre-election likely voter (LV) polls did not factor in the heavy turnout of new Kerry voters. The final pre-election NY poll had a 4% margin of error (MoE). There was a 95% probability that Kerry would be in the 54.5-62.5% range – and that is conservative because it is based on an LV poll.

The NY exit poll had a 3.2% MoE. Therefore, there was a 95% probability that Kerry's vote was between 60.9-67.3% and was within the MoE of both the LV pre-election poll (which low-balled Kerry turnout) and the unadjusted exit poll.

4 - Bush supposedly did better than his 2000 vote share in the 15 largest (Democratic) New York City and suburban counties. It's an Urban Legend – impossible on its face.

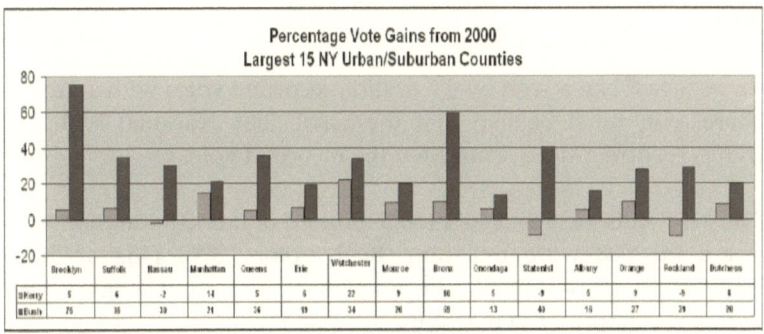

35 - Myth: Unlike touch screens and optical scanners, lever voting machines cannot be programmed to switch votes. The NY exit poll was off by 12%.

Fact: The levers did not produce paper ballots; vote counts could not be verified. Defective levers were placed in urban precincts; many voters left the precincts without voting. Lever advocates refuse to consider this fact: Votes CAST on levers were COUNTED on unverifiable central tabulators.

36-Myth: Polling data was cherry-picked and biased for Kerry.

Fact: The following models used exit poll data for 1250 precincts provided by Edison-Mitofsky. The data included partisan response rates and corresponding average within precinct discrepancies (WPE).

The models produced equivalent results. They confirmed the USCV simulation which debunked the reluctant Bush responder (rBr) hypothesis.

a) 1250 precinct response optimizer: Kerry won: 52.1-47.9%.
b) Location-size response: Kerry won this category by 52.1-47.9%.
c) State exit poll response: Kerry won by 52.3-47.7%.
d) National Exit Poll (13660 respondents: Kerry by 51.7-47.0%
e) State exit polls (76,000 respondents): Kerry by 51.1-47.9%.

158

2008 anomalies

To believe Obama won by 9.5 million recorded votes with a 52.9% share, you must believe that the Final 2008 National Exit Poll (NEP) is correct since it matched the recorded vote.

The NEP indicated that 46% (60.5 million) of the 131.4 million who voted in 2008 were returning Bush voters; 37% (48.6 million) returning Kerry voters. An impossible 103% turnout of 2004 Bush voters was required to match the recorded vote.

There had to be 12 million more returning Bush than Kerry voters. The NEP implied that Bush won in 2004 by 52.6-42.3%, but the recorded vote was 50.7-48.3%. And Kerry won the 2004 unadjusted state exit polls by 52-47%.

You must believe that the 2008 and 2004 unadjusted state and national exit polls were wrong even though Obama won the state exit polls by 58.0-40.5% – a 23 million vote margin.

He won the unadjusted NEP by 61-37%. Of the 17,836 respondents, 4,178 were asked who they voted for in 2004: 43.4% said Kerry and 38.6% said Bush. Obama's 58.0% exit poll share was confirmed using these percentages as a basis for calculating returning voters.

You must believe the True Vote Model TVM) was wrong even though it was the third confirmation of Obama's 58.0% exit poll share. It used Final 2008 NEP vote shares, combined with a realistic, plausible return voter mix (based on Kerry's True Vote) which replaced the impossible Final NEP mix.

The TVM sensitivity analysis shows that Obama won the worst case scenario by 19.5 million votes and a 56.7% share (he had 67% of new voters and 15% of returning Bush voters). Obama had a 58.0% True Vote share in the most-likely base case scenario based on his Final NEP 72% share of new voters and 17% share of returning Bush voters.

You must believe there is nothing suspicious about the fact that Obama had 52.3% of 121 million votes counted on Election Day and 59.2% of the final 10 million late (paper ballot) votes recorded after Election Day.

According to the Final 2008 NEP, returning 2004 third-party voters comprised 5.2 million (4%) of the electorate. But only 1.2 million third-party votes were recorded in 2004. This anomaly indicates that third party votes were uncounted and/or switched.

You must disregard the unadjusted 2008 NEP in which 43.4% of 1,815 respondents said they voted for Kerry and 38.6% said Bush.

You must overlook the fact that to match the recorded vote, the number of Kerry respondents was reduced to 1,546 (-14.8%) while Bush respondents increased by 19.2%.

Vote Swing vs. Exit Poll Red-Shift

After the 2004 election, exit poll naysayers claimed that the near-zero correlation between Swing (the change in Bush vote share from 2000 to 2004) and the 2004 Exit Poll Red shift (discrepancy) "kills the fraud argument".

The pollsters provided a swing vs. red-shift scatter chart of 1250 precincts. They pointed to the flat (zero slope) regression line as evidence that the election was not fraudulent. They implied that a positively sloped regression would have indicated fraud.

But they were wrong to use 2000 and 2004 recorded vote data as the baseline in calculating swing. If they had used the 2000 and 2004 unadjusted exit polls as the baseline, it would have proved the 2004 election was fraudulent – by their definition.

The exit pollster's initial explanation for the discrepancies was that non-response bias skewed the exit polls – the so-called reluctant Bush responder (rBr). When that argument was refuted, they tried "Swing vs. Red shift". Finally, "False Recall" was promoted to explain the impossible number of returning Bush 2000 voters implied by the 2004 National Exit Poll. In each case, the recorded votes were used as the baseline, rather than total votes cast. Uncounted votes and an estimate of the True Vote were ignored.

The pollsters used bogus 2000 and 2004 recorded exit poll precinct data to prove that there was no fraud in 2004 – a circular argument if there ever was one. There were nearly six million uncounted votes in 2000 and four million in 2004. That fact alone is proof that the True Vote differed from the recorded vote in both elections.

Using recorded vote swing as the basis to "prove" that the 2004 election was fraud-free was misleading disinformation. It was meant to cast doubt on the state and national exit polls which indicated that Kerry had 51-52%.

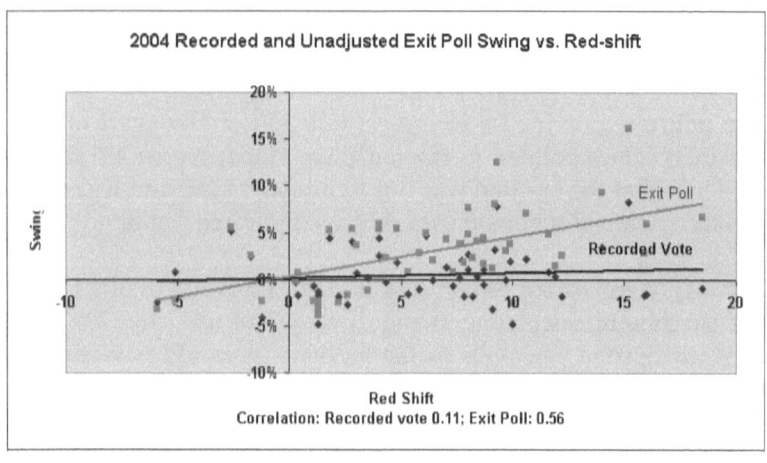

However, when unadjusted 2000 and 2004 state exit polls are used as a proxy for the True Vote, there is a strong positive correlation.

In other words, Swing is now defined as the change in the 2-party unadjusted state exit poll share from the previous election. Red-shift is the difference between the 2-party unadjusted state exit poll and the recorded share in the current election.

In the 2004 Exit Poll Evaluation Report, pollsters Edison-Mitofsky data refuted their "Zero slope = No fraud". The WPE (Within Precinct Error) correlation matrix showed a relatively high 0.48 correlation for 2000-2004. It was just .05 for 1996-2000.

The table indicates that 1992 and 2004 elections (Bush 1 and 2 were incumbents) were fraudulent, while the 1996 and 2000 elections (Clinton was the incumbent) were fair. Actually, unadjusted 2000 election exit poll data shows that it was very fraudulent. In the 1988-2008 presidential elections, Democrats won the average unadjusted exit polls by 52-42%. They won the recorded vote by 48-46%.

Edison-Mitofsky WPE Correlation
(2004 Exit Poll Evaluation Report)

Year	2000	1996	1992	1988
2004	0.48	0.19	0.35	0.30
2000	-	0.05	0.12	0.23
1996	-	-	0.15	0.26
1992	-	-	-	0.29

Swing vs. Red-shift correlation

Method	1992	1996	2000	2004	2008	Average
Recorded	0.09	0.06	0.20	0.16	0.14	0.01
Exit Poll	0.65	0.10	0.57	0.62	0.38	0.47

To use the fraudulent recorded vote as a basis for calculating swing and then claim that the near-zero correlation "kills the fraud argument" is a logical fallacy. Elections can be fraudulent or fraud-free regardless of the correlation. The scatter graphs below kill the naysayer 2004 Swing/ Red shift "no slope, no fraud" canard.

In the 1988-2008 elections, Democratic presidential candidates did nearly 8% better in unadjusted exit polls (52-42%) than in the recorded vote (48-46%). The discrepancies were due to a combination of uncounted votes and electronic vote switching. The uncounted vote rate trend has declined, but electronic vote switching has more than taken up the slack.

The National Election Pool (NEP) mainstream media consortium has never released unadjusted precinct exit poll data. Their transparent claim is the need for exit poll respondent confidentiality. It's a misleading canard; exit poll respondents do not reveal personal information.

In their 2004 report, the pollsters provided average Within Precinct Error (WPE) statistics for the 1988-2004 exit polls. That report provided more than enough historical information to hoist the NEP, the pollsters and the naysayers on their own petard.

1988-2004: Uncounted Votes and Exit Poll discrepancies

Uncounted Votes have steadily declined as a percent of total votes cast – from 10.4% in 1988 to 2.7% in 2004. When added to the recorded vote in order to derive the total votes cast for the five elections from 1988-2004, the average Democratic unadjusted exit poll share is within 0.1% of the adjusted vote. Comparing the adjusted vote to the aggregate exit poll and recorded vote:

Democrat	Record	Exit	2-party	Adjusted
Average	46.9	48.8	52.7	48.9
1988 Dukakis	45.6	46.8	47.3	48.7
1992 Clinton	43.0	45.7	56.8	45.7
1996 Clinton	49.2	50.2	55.8	51.4
2000 Gore	48.4	49.4	51.4	49.7
2004 Kerry	48.3	51.8	52.3	49.0

In each of the last five elections the unadjusted Democratic exit poll share exceeded the recorded vote. But which of the five stands out from the rest? The 2004 exit poll discrepancies were different in kind and scope from those of the prior four elections. Unlike 1988-2000, the 2004 discrepancies cannot be explained by uncounted votes alone.

There are some exit poll critics who claim that the large 1992 exit poll discrepancy proves that 2004 exit polls which indicate that the election was stolen are "crap" and "bad science". After all, they say, there were no allegations of fraud in 1992. They fail to mention (or are unaware of) the fact that in 1992 Clinton beat Bush by a recorded 43.6-38.0m but 9.4m votes were uncounted – and 70-80% were Democratic. When the uncounted votes are added, the adjusted vote becomes 50.7-40.3m (45.7-36.4%), which exactly matched Clinton's unadjusted exit poll.

From 1988-2000, after the uncounted adjustment, there was a 0.85% average Democratic exit poll discrepancy and 2.9 WPE. In 2004, after the uncounted vote adjustment, there was a 2.8% discrepancy and Bush's margin was reduced from 3.0 to 1.3 million. But uncounted votes were only one component of Election Fraud 2004.

2000-2008 Late Vote Anomalies

In the last 3 elections, the average Democratic late vote share was 7% higher than the vote share recorded on Election Day.

On Election Day 2000, 102.6 million votes were recorded; Gore led by 48.3-48.1% (50.1% of the 2-party vote), but had 55.6% of the 2.7 million late 2-party votes, an 11.0% increase in margin. There were 6 million uncounted votes.

On Election Day 2004, 116.7 million votes were recorded. Bush led by 51.2-48.3%. But Kerry had 54.2% of the 4.8 million late 2-party votes, a 10.4% increase in margin.

There were 4 million uncounted votes. Late votes (absentees, etc.) became irrelevant when Bush was declared the winner. The media reported that Bush won by 3.5m votes; they still quote that initial margin today. Edison-Mitofsky matched the Final Exit Poll to the initial Election Day votes.

Assuming that Kerry's 53.0% late vote share was representative of the 122.3m recorded total, his vote total is 64.8m. Adding his 75% share of the 3.4m documented uncounted votes brings his final total to 67.4m (53.5%), matching the True Vote Model. The model assumed total votes cast in 2000, a 5% voter mortality rate and 98% turnout of 2000 voters in 2004. The 12:22am Composite NEP vote shares were used in the calculation.

There was a 0.72 correlation between the late state vote shares and the exit polls. For states which had more than 40k late votes, the correlation was a strong 0.93.

The evidence that the "pristine" exit polls were close to the True Vote is confirmed by:

1) high correlation between state exit polls and late vote shares
2) small discrepancies between the exit polls and late vote shares
3) consistent pattern of high Kerry late shares compared to Election Day

How does one explain the discrepancies between the initial and late recorded state vote shares? Kerry's late vote exceeded his initial share in 38 states (15 of 19 battleground states).

Corresponding vote discrepancies were significant in the East but near zero in the Far West, strongly suggesting election fraud in early-reporting, vote-rich battleground states. A false impression was created that Bush was winning the popular vote while the state and national exit polls indicated that Kerry was winning big.

In the Far Western states there was virtually no difference between the 15.6 million initial and 3.3 million late recorded vote shares. Kerry was a steady 53% winner.

But the Far West average exit poll WPE was 6.4%, indicating a 56% Kerry share. Was vote-padding in effect?

Not one media pundit has ever noted the following:
1) All exit polls are adjusted to match the recorded vote.
2) The National Exit Poll implied a 110% Bush 2000 voter turnout
3) Unadjusted state exit polls were close to the True Vote.
4) The final 5 million recorded votes were close to the True Vote.

2008: The Final 10 million late recorded votes

On Election Day 2008, 121.2 million votes were recorded. Obama led by 63.4-56.1 million (52.3-46.3%). There were 10.2 million votes recorded after Election Day. Obama won the late votes by 59.2-37.5%. The final recorded vote: 69.5-59.9m (52.87-45.62%).

It is logical to assume that the late votes were accurate because
1) They were cast using paper ballots, not unverifiable DREs
2) Obama was declared the winner on Election Day, so there was nothing to gain by manipulating the votes recorded afterwards.

The unadjusted exit poll discrepancies from the recorded vote were far beyond the 1.2% exit poll margin of error. But the polls were generally very close to the late recorded vote shares. T

he largest deviations were in states where there were a relatively small number of late votes – as would be expected. Assuming the late votes were fairly representative of the total state electorate, they can be viewed as super exit polls having thousands more respondents than actual polls where 1000-2500 voters are interviewed.

Obama won the state unadjusted exit poll aggregate by 58.0-40.5% – a close match to his 59.2% late recorded share. There were 83,000 respondents. He had 58.0% in the True Vote Model.

The National Exit Poll (17,836 respondents) is a subset of the state polls. Obama won the unadjusted NEP by a 61-37% margin. He had 58.0% share in the True Vote Model.

APPENDIX A: Basic Mathematics

The **Law of Large Numbers** is the bedrock of statistical analysis and the basis for polling analysis. As the number of observations in a survey increases, the average (mean) of the sample will approach the theoretical population mean.

Consider coin flipping. As the number of flips increase, the average percentage of heads will approach 50%. As the sample-size of an unbiased poll increases, the averages will closely approach the expected vote shares – in theory.

Descriptive statistics: summarizes data in tables and graphs
Inferential statistics: estimates the characteristics of the data
Probability: likelihood of an event (0-100%).

Sample-size: number of respondents surveyed in a poll
Mean: average of the poll sample
Median: central value of the sample
Mode: most frequent value occurring in the sample
Variance: measure of poll volatility (spread) from the mean
Standard deviation: square root of the variance
Population mean: actual vote share
Confidence level: probability poll includes the population mean
Confidence interval: range of values containing population mean
Margin of Error: the width of the confidence interval (e.g. +/- 3%)
Correlation: a measure of the degree of association (-1 to +1) between two sets of data. If zero, there is no correlation.

Binomial distribution

Calculates the probability P that a given number of events (successes) will occur in n trials where each trial has a constant probability p of success. For instance, the probability of flipping heads (a success) is 50%.

The binomial distribution is used in problems with a fixed number of tests or trials, where the outcome of any trial is a success or failure.

The trials are independent. The probability of success is constant in each trial (heads or tails, win or lose).

1988-2008: 274 state exit polls

The probability that the margin of error would be exceeded at the 95% level of confidence is 5%. Therefore, approximately 5% (14) of the 274 presidential state exit polls from 1988-2008 would be expected to exceed the margin of error, approximately 7 for the Republican and 7 for the Democrat.

Example: Calculate the probability P that at least 55 of 57 exit polls would flip from the Democrats in the polls to Republicans in the vote.

Note that the probability that *at least* 55 exit polls would flip is *1-the probability that 54 or fewer would flip*. Therefore the probability is given by the **Binomial distribution**:

P = 1-Binomdist (54, 57, .5, true)
P = 1.13E-14 = 0.000000000000011 or 1 in 88 trillion!

Republicans did better in the recorded vote than the exit poll in 226 (82.4%) elections. **The probability of this one-sided shift is 3.7E-31 or 1 in 2.7 million trillion trillion.**

Poisson distribution
Approximates the Binomial if the number (n) of trials is large and the probability (p) of a success is low.

Example: Calculate the probability that in the 1988-2008 presidential elections, the margin of error would be exceeded in 123 of 274 state exit polls for the Republicans.

P = Poisson (123, .025*274, false)

P = 1 in 1.8 billion trillion trillion trillion trillion trillion trillion trillion trillion. There are 106 places to the right of the decimal!

Normal Distribution
Used throughout statistics, natural sciences, and social sciences as a simple model for complex systems.

Example: Calculate the probability Kerry would win Ohio. In the exit poll (1963 sample) he led by 54.25-45.75% (2-party).

1: Calculate the margin of error
MoE = 2.21% = 1.96 * sqrt (p * (1-p)/n) where p=.5425, n=1963
Add a 20% cluster factor. The adjusted MoE = 2.65%;

2: Calculate the standard deviation for the NORMDIST function
Stdev = .0135 = .0265 / 1.96

3: Calculate the probability P that Kerry had at least 50%.
P = 99.9% = NORMDIST (.5425, .5, .0135, true)

Monte Carlo Electoral Vote Simulation

1. Calculate the projected 2-party vote share V (i) for each state.
V (i) = poll share plus undecided voter allocation:
V (i) = PS (i) + UVA (i), where i=1, 51 states

2. Calculate the probability of winning each state given the projected share and margin of error at the 95% confidence level:

P (i) = NORMDIST (V (i), 0.5, MoE / 1.96, true).

The theoretical expected electoral vote is the summation of 51 state win probabilities times the electoral votes:

EV = $\sum$ P (i) * EV (i), for i = 1, 51

In each election trial, a random number between zero and one is generated for each state and compared to the state win probability. If RND > P (i), candidate A wins the state; if less, candidate B wins. The candidate with at least 270 electoral votes is the winner.

The mean electoral vote is the average of the n trials. As n increases, the mean will approach the expected theoretical value calculated by the summation formula The EV win probability is equal to the number of election trial wins divided by the total election trials.

APPENDIX B: Historical Presidential Elections

Election		1988	1992	1996	2000	2004	2008
Votes Cast		102.2	113.9	105.0	110.8	125.7	131.4
Recorded		91.6	104.4	96.3	105.4	122.3	131.1
Net Uncounted		10.6	9.5	8.7	5.4	3.4	0.3
Recorded Vote (%)	**Avg**						
Democrat	47.9	45.7	43.0	49.3	48.4	48.3	52.9
Republican	45.9	53.4	37.4	40.7	47.9	50.7	45.6
Margin	2.0	-7.7	5.6	8.6	0.5	-2.4	7.3
Democratic Exit Poll							
National	51.6	49.8	46.3	52.6	48.5	51.7	61.0
State	51.7	50.3	47.6	52.6	50.8	51.1	58.0
True Vote	53.0	50.2	51.1	53.6	51.5	53.6	58.0
State Exit Poll Aggregate							
Sample-size (000)	62.5	34.0	54.4	69.7	58.2	76.2	82.4
Democrat	51.7	50.3	47.6	52.6	50.8	51.1	58.0
Republican	41.6	48.7	31.7	37.1	44.4	47.5	40.3
Exit Poll Margin	**10.1**	**1.6**	**15.9**	**15.5**	**6.4**	**3.6**	**17.7**
Margin of Error							
Average	3.3%	3.3%	3.4%	3.1%	3.6%	3.1%	3.0%
Red-shift to GOP	226	20	44	43	34	40	45
States Exceed MoE	126	11	26	16	13	23	37
Exceed MoE (GOP)	123	11	26	16	12	22	36
National Exit Poll							
Sample-size (000)	14.3	11.6	15.2	NA	13.1	13.7	17.8
Democrat	51.6	49.8	46.3	52.6	48.5	51.7	61.0
Republican	41.7	49.1	33.5	37.1	46.3	47.0	37.2
Exit Poll Margin	**9.9**	**0.6**	**12.8**	**15.5**	**2.2**	**4.7**	**23.8**
State Exit Poll (WPD)							
Democrat	50.7	49.3	45.7	50.2	49.4	51.9	58.0
Republican	43.1	49.7	34.7	39.8	46.9	47.1	40.5
Exit Poll Margin	**7.6**	**-0.4**	**11.0**	**10.4**	**2.5**	**4.8**	**17.5**
True Vote Model							
Democrat	53.0	50.2	51.1	53.6	51.5	53.6	58.0
Republican	41.0	48.8	30.4	36.5	44.7	45.1	40.4
True Vote Margin	**12.0**	**1.4**	**20.7**	**17.1**	**6.8**	**8.5**	**17.6**

1988-2008 Presidential Vote Shares

Measure	Dem	Rep	Margin	Basis
1) Recorded	47.9	45.9	2.0	Vote count
2) WPE / IMS	50.8	43.1	7.7	Edison-Mitofsky
3) State Exit	51.8	41.6	10.2	Roper archive
4) National Exit	51.7	41.7	10.0	Roper archive
5) True Vote 1	50.2	43.8	6.4	Previous recorded vote
6) True Vote 2	51.6	42.5	9.1	Previous votes cast
7) True Vote 3	52.5	41.5	11.0	Previous unadjusted exit poll
8) True Vote 4	53.0	41.0	12.0	Previous True Vote

True Vote Model Method	Avg	1988	1992	1996	2000	2004	2008
1 Recorded Vote	50.2	48.6	48.8	48.4	48.5	52.3	54.5
2 Votes Cast	51.6	50.6	50.3	50.0	50.0	53.3	55.2
3 Exit Poll	52.5	50.6	51.2	51.6	50.9	54.3	56.4
4 True Vote	53.0	50.2	51.1	53.6	51.5	53.6	58.0

2-party Exit Poll							
Democrat	56.57	50.8	60.0	58.6	53.4	51.8	59.0
Republican	43.43	49.2	40.0	41.4	46.6	48.2	41.0

Correlation: Recorded Swing vs. EP Shift						
Red-shift	Avg	1992	1996	2000	2004	2008
Recorded	0.01	-0.09	0.06	0.20	-0.16	-0.14
Exit Poll	0.46	-0.65	0.10	0.57	0.62	0.38
E/M (WPE)	0.24	-0.29	0.15	0.05	0.48	-

1988-2008 State Exit Polls Exceeding the Margin of Error

MoE is the average margin of error for the 6 elections, CF is the cluster factor, and N is the number of exit polls in which the MoE was exceeded.

MoE	CF	N	Probability	
2.5%	0%	157	E-106	ZERO
3.2%	30%	126	E-75	ZERO (base case cluster factor)
3.7%	50%	113	E-62	ZERO
5.0%	100%	76	E-31	ZERO
6.2%	150%	50	E-14	1 in 40 trillion
7.0%	180%	35	E-7	1 in 1.5 million
7.5%	200%	25	2E-3	1 in 500

The following table lists
a) States (n) in which the exit poll shifted to the Republican
b) Number of states which red-shifted beyond the margin of error
c) Probability of states red-shifting beyond the MoE
d) Democratic unadjusted aggregate state exit poll share
e) Democratic recorded share
f) Difference between Democratic exit poll and recorded share

Year	N	MoE	Prob	ExitP	Vote	Diff	
1988	20	11	E-11	50.3	45.7	4.6	Dukakis may have won
1992	44	26	E-25	47.6	43.0	4.6	Clinton landslide
1996	43	16	E-13	52.6	49.3	3.3	Clinton landslide
2000	34	12	E-09	50.8	48.4	2.4	Gore win stolen
2004	40	22	E-20	51.1	48.3	2.8	Kerry landslide stolen
2008	45	36	E-37	58.0	52.9	5.1	Obama landslide denied
Total	226	123	E-106	51.7	47.9	3.8	123 of 126 red-shift

2004 Party ID

	Pct	Kerry	Bush	Other	Pct	Kerry	Bush	Other
Democrat	38.8%	91%	9%	0%	37%	90%	10%	0%
Republican	35.1%	8%	92%	0%	37%	7%	93%	0%
Independent	26.1%	52%	43%	5%	26%	47.6%	48.6%	3.8%
Share	100%	51.7%	47.0%	1.3%	100%	48.3%	50.7%	1.0%
Votes	125.7	66.0	59.1	1.6	122.3	59.0	62.0	1.2

2004 Bush Approval

	Rating	Kerry	Bush
Final NEP			
Approve	53%	9.5%	89.5%
Disapprove	47%	92.0%	7.0%
Share	100%	48.3%	50.7%
Votes (mil)	122.3	67.5	56.9
Unadjusted Exit Poll			
Approve	50.3%	9%	90%
Disapprove	49.7%	95%	4%
Share	100%	51.7%	47.3%
Votes	122.3	63.3	57.8
Pre-election Polls			
Approve	48%	9%	90%
Disapprove	52%	95%	4%
Share	100%	53.7%	45.3%
Votes	125.7	67.5	56.9

APPENDIX C: Unadjusted and Final National Exit Polls

2008	Mix	Unadjusted Obama	McCain	Other	Mix	Adjusted Final Obama	McCain	Other	Turnout
DNV	13.4%	71%	27%	2%	13%	71%	27%	2%	-
Kerry	43.4%	89%	9%	2%	37%	89%	9%	2%	87%
Bush	38.6%	17%	82%	1%	46%	17%	82%	1%	103%
Other	4.5%	72%	26%	2%	4%	72%	26%	2%	452%
Total	100%	58.0%	40.3%	1.7%	100%	52.9%	45.6%	1.5%	
Votes	131.47	76.25	53.04	2.18	131.47	69.50	59.95	2.02	

2004	Mix	Kerry	Bush	Other	Mix	Kerry	Bush	Other	
DNV	18.4%	57%	41%	2%	17%	54%	44%	2%	-
Gore	38.4%	91%	8%	1%	37%	90%	10%	0%	93%
Bush	39.5%	10%	90%	0%	43%	9%	91%	0%	110%
Other	3.7%	64%	17%	19%	3%	64%	14%	22%	98%
Total	100%	51.7%	46.8%	1.5%	100%	48.3%	50.7%	1.0%	
Votes	125.7	65.1	58.8	1.84	122.3	59.0	62.0	1.2	

2000	Mix	Gore	Bush	Other	Mix	Gore	Bush	Other	
DNV	16%	52%	43%	5%	18%	52%	43%	5%	-
Clinton	44%	87%	10%	3%	40%	87%	10%	3%	94%
Dole	32%	7%	91%	2%	34%	7%	91%	2%	96%
Perot	8%	23%	65%	12%	8%	23%	65%	12%	92%
Total	100%	50.7%	45.6%	3.7%	100%	48.4%	47.9%	3.7%	
Votes	110.8	56.2	50.5	4.1	105.5	51.00	50.46	4.00	

1996	Mix	Clinton	Dole	Other	Mix	Clinton	Dole	Other	
DNV	14%	55%	31%	14%	13%	55%	33%	12%	-
Clinton	42%	85%	9%	6%	38%	85%	9%	6%	86%
Bush	27%	14%	81%	5%	31%	13%	82%	5%	80%
Perot	17%	32%	42%	26%	18%	32%	42%	26%	89%
Total	100%	52.6%	37.2%	10.2%	100%	49.2%	40.7%	10.1%	
Votes	105.0	55.3	39.0	10.7	96.3	47.4	39.2	9.7	

1992	Mix	Clinton	Bush	Other	Mix	Clinton	Bush	Other	
DNV	18%	46%	25%	29%	18%	46%	25%	29%	-
Dukakis	36%	83%	5%	12%	28%	83%	5%	12%	74%
Bush	45%	21%	59%	20%	53%	21%	59%	20%	119%
Other	1%	32%	30%	38%	1%	32%	30%	38%	86%
Total	100%	47.9%	33.2%	18.9%	100%	43.0%	37.5%	19.5%	
Votes	113.8	54.6	37.7	21.5	104.4	44.9	39.1	20.4	

1988	Mix	Dukakis	Bush	Other	Mix	Dukakis	Bush	Other	
DNV	11%	57%	42%	1%	8%	47%	52%	1%	-
Mondale	34%	95%	4%	1%	33%	92%	7%	1%	85%
Reagan	54%	20%	79%	1%	58%	19%	80%	1%	103%
Other	1%	50%	49%	1%	1%	50%	49%	1%	93%
Total	100%	49.9%	49.1%	1.0%	100%	45.6%	53.4%	1.0%	
Votes	102.2	51.0	50.2	1.0	91.6	41.8	48.9	0.9	

2008	Cast	MoE	BO	JM	Diff	EV	BO	JM	Diff	EV
APPENDIX D				2008 Exit Poll			Recorded Vote			
Total	131.15	2.9	58	40.3	17.7	420	52.87	45.6	7.25	365
AK	304	3.7	49.1	47.5	1.6	3	37.9	59.4	-21.5	
AL	2,126	3.9	52	47	5.0	9	38.7	60.3	-21.6	
AR	1,092	4	46	50.6	-4.6		38.9	58.7	-19.8	
AZ	2,497	3.6	51.4	47.9	3.5	10	44.9	53.4	-8.5	
CA	13,828	2.5	67	30.6	36.4	55	61	36.9	24.1	55
CO	2,308	3.6	51.9	46.1	5.8	9	53.7	44.7	9.0	7
CT	1,610	3.8	73.4	24	49.4	7	60.6	38.2	22.4	9
DC	306	3.1	92	6.4	85.6	3	92.5	6.5	86.0	21
DE	408	4.3	68.6	30.9	37.7	3	61.9	36.9	25.0	7
FL	7,951	2.2	52.1	46.1	6.0	27	50.9	48.1	2.8	4
GA	4,183	2.9	51.1	48.7	2.4	15	46.9	52.1	-5.2	3
HI	457	3.9	70.4	27.6	42.8	4	71.8	26.6	45.2	
IA	1,501	2.3	56.9	41.2	15.7	7	53.9	44.4	9.5	3
ID	644	4.5	41.8	55.9	-14.1		36	61.3	-25.3	27
IL	5,436	3.2	66.3	32.4	33.9	21	61.9	36.8	25.1	
IN	2,758	2.6	55.7	43.2	12.5	11	49.9	48.9	1.0	4
KS	1,219	4.5	46.1	52.6	-6.5		41.6	56.5	-14.9	7
KY	1,952	3.3	46.8	51.6	-4.8		41.1	57.4	-16.3	
LA	2,149	3	45.9	53	-7.1		39.9	58.6	-18.7	21
MA	3,044	4.3	67	29.6	37.4	12	61.8	36	25.8	11
MD	2,611	3.8	67.2	30.7	36.5	10	61.9	36.5	25.4	
ME	716	3.1	62.1	35.4	26.7	4	57.7	40.4	17.3	
MI	4,865	2.2	62.2	35.5	26.7	17	57.4	40.9	16.5	
MN	2,759	2.5	61.9	35.9	26.0	10	54.1	43.8	10.3	12
MO	2,846	2.4	57.5	41.4	16.1	11	49.3	49.4	-0.1	10
MS	1,439	3.9	48.4	51.1	-2.7		43	56.2	-13.2	4
MT	473	3.5	54.4	44	10.4	3	47.2	49.4	-2.2	17
NC	4,370	2.4	53.5	45.8	7.7	15	49.7	49.4	0.3	10
ND	321	4.1	38.9	59	-20.1		44.5	53.1	-8.6	
NE	844	3.8	49.2	49.1	0.1	5	41.6	56.5	-14.9	
NH	708	2.6	61.6	37.1	24.5	4	54.1	44.5	9.6	
NJ	3,637	3.1	63.8	35.1	28.7	15	57.2	41.6	15.6	15
NM	846	2.4	58.8	39.5	19.3	5	56.9	41.8	15.1	
NV	1,027	2.4	56.3	41.8	14.5	5	55.1	42.7	12.4	
NY	7,559	2.9	71.5	27.3	44.2	31	62.8	36.1	26.7	
OH	5,483	2.2	56.3	42	14.3	20	51.4	46.8	4.6	1
OK	1,507	4.2	40.6	59.3	-18.7		34.4	65.6	-31.2	4
OR	1,818	3.6	58.4	38.6	19.8	7	56.7	40.4	16.3	
PA	5,747	2.3	63.8	35.3	28.5	21	54.5	44.2	10.3	15
RI	507	4.1	67.5	29.4	38.1	4	63.1	35.2	27.9	5
SC	2,100	3.7	47.5	51.4	-3.9		44.9	53.9	-9.0	
SD	390	4.1	48.7	48.7	0.0		44.7	53.2	-8.5	13
TN	2,516	3.1	47.7	50.3	-2.6		41.8	56.9	-15.1	5
TX	8,435	2.8	46.2	52.3	-6.1		43.6	55.4	-11.8	3
UT	939	5	31.5	63.8	-32.3		34.3	62.3	-28.0	11
VA	3,650	2.5	62.5	36.7	25.8	13	52.6	46.3	6.3	31
VT	308	3.9	71.5	26.5	45.0	3	67.5	30.5	37.0	20
WA	3,073	3.6	57.9	38.2	19.7	11	57.4	40.3	17.1	10
WI	2,887	2.4	63.3	35.7	27.6	10	56.2	42.3	13.9	
WV	741	3.9	45.1	53.1	-8.0		42.6	55.7	-13.1	
WY	250	3.9	34.1	64.2	-30.1		32.5	64.8	-32.3	

2004	Cast	MoE	Kerry	Bush	Diff	EV	Kerry	Bush	Diff	EV
Total	125,736	3.1	51.0	47.7	3.4	349	48.27	50.7	-2.5	252
AK	293	3.7	44.7	51.9	-7.2		35.5	61.1	-25.6	
AL	2,851	4.6	39.7	59.1	-19.4		36.8	62.5	-25.7	
AR	1,140	3.3	44.4	54.8	-10.4		44.5	54.3	-9.8	
AZ	2,239	2.9	46.3	52.8	-6.6		44.4	54.9	-10.5	
CA	12,807	2.6	53.9	44.2	9.7	55	54.3	44.4	9.9	55
CO	2,097	2.5	49.3	49.2	0.1	9	47.0	51.7	-4.7	
CT	1,524	4.2	62.5	36.0	26.5	7	54.3	43.9	10.4	7
DC	270	2.5	90.7	8.1	82.6	3	89.2	9.3	79.9	3
DE	385	4.4	63.3	36.0	27.3	3	53.3	45.8	7.5	3
FL	7,372	2.4	50.8	48.0	2.8	27	47.1	52.1	-5.0	
GA	3,332	3.1	41.8	57.4	-15.6		41.4	58.0	-16.6	
HI	433	5.0	61.3	38.7	22.5	4	54.0	45.3	8.7	4
IA	1,522	2.5	49.3	49.0	0.3	7	49.2	49.9	-0.7	
ID	585	4.1	27.8	70.3	-42.4		30.3	68.4	-38.1	
IL	5,672	3.3	56.0	43.3	12.7	21	54.8	44.5	10.3	21
IN	2,598	4.1	39.5	59.5	-20.0		39.3	59.9	-20.6	
KS	1,188	4.7	34.2	64.6	-30.4		36.6	62.0	-25.4	
KY	1,930	3.9	42.4	56.1	-13.7		39.7	59.6	-19.9	
LA	2,067	3.1	44.2	54.5	-10.3		42.2	56.7	-14.5	
MA	3,085	4.0	64.7	33.1	31.6	12	61.9	36.8	25.1	12
MD	2,413	3.9	54.8	43.8	11.1	10	55.9	42.9	13.0	10
ME	736	2.8	55.4	42.3	13.1	4	53.6	44.6	9.0	4
MI	4,818	2.5	53.9	44.7	9.1	17	51.2	47.8	3.4	17
MN	2,887	2.7	56.3	42.4	13.9	10	51.1	47.6	3.5	10
MO	2,815	2.7	50.4	48.7	1.7	11	46.1	53.3	-7.2	
MS	1,263	4.5	45.6	53.7	-8.1		39.8	59.4	-19.6	
MT	482	5.0	39.3	56.7	-17.4		38.6	59.1	-20.5	
NC	3,639	2.7	46.1	53.0	-6.9		43.6	56.0	-12.4	
ND	330	4.5	31.4	66.8	-35.4		35.5	62.9	-27.4	
NE	793	4.4	36.4	62.4	-26.0		32.7	65.9	-33.2	
NH	677	2.9	56.7	42.0	14.8	4	50.2	48.9	1.3	4
NJ	3,693	3.2	59.1	38.6	20.6	15	52.9	46.2	6.7	15
NM	837	2.8	53.9	44.3	9.6	5	49.0	49.8	-0.8	
NV	871	2.7	52.4	46.5	6.0	5	47.9	50.5	-2.6	
NY	7,698	3.2	62.1	36.2	25.9	31	58.4	40.1	18.3	31
OH	5,485	2.8	54.1	45.7	8.3	20	48.7	50.8	-2.1	
OK	1,541	3.1	36.3	62.6	-26.4		34.4	65.6	-31.2	
OR	1,924	4.0	52.2	46.3	5.9	7	51.3	47.2	4.1	7
PA	5,845	2.7	56.6	42.9	13.7	21	50.9	48.4	2.5	21
RI	467	4.3	63.3	34.5	28.8	4	59.4	38.7	20.7	4
SC	1,899	3.0	47.8	50.6	-2.9		40.9	58.0	-17.1	
SD	378	3.1	35.1	62.6	-27.5		38.4	59.9	-21.5	
TN	2,319	3.0	41.6	56.4	-14.8		42.5	56.8	-14.3	
TX	7,950	3.0	41.5	57.5	-16.0		38.2	61.1	-22.9	
UT	1,022	4.3	31.5	66.3	-34.8		26.0	71.5	-45.5	
VA	3,134	3.4	52.7	46.8	5.9	13	45.5	53.7	-8.2	
VT	316	4.4	68.8	27.8	41.0	3	58.9	38.8	20.1	3
WA	2,851	2.7	56.5	41.9	14.6	11	52.8	45.6	7.2	11
WI	3,010	2.6	52.0	46.8	5.2	10	49.7	49.3	0.4	10
WV	798	3.0	41.7	56.9	-15.2		43.2	56.1	-12.9	
WY	247	4.2	28.9	68.2	-39.3		29.1	68.9	-39.8	

2000	Cast	MoE	Gore	Bush	Diff	EV	Gore	Bush	Diff	EV
Total	110,825	3.4	50.7	44.5	6.2	408	48.4	47.9	0.5	267
AK	270	4.4	31.0	56.0	-25.0		27.7	58.6	-31.0	
AL	1,953	4.4	51.7	46.2	5.5	9	41.6	56.5	-14.9	
AR	936	3.8	52.2	44.4	7.8	6	45.9	51.3	-5.4	
AZ	1,644	3.7	47.1	46.4	0.8	10	44.7	51.0	-6.3	
CA	11,489	2.4	53.9	39.6	14.3	55	53.4	41.7	11.8	55
CO	1,633	4.2	45.3	44.9	0.4	9	42.4	50.8	-8.4	
CT	1,332	3.8	54.8	37.7	17.1	7	55.9	38.4	17.5	7
DC	267	3.2	84.1	10.7	73.5	3	85.2	9.0	76.2	3
DE	352	4.0	58.8	37.5	21.3	3	55.0	41.9	13.1	3
FL	6,006	3.0	53.4	43.6	9.7	27	48.8	48.8	0.0	
GA	2,827	3.6	49.2	46.7	2.6	15	43.0	54.7	-11.7	
HI	340	4.4	52.2	40.0	12.2	4	55.8	37.5	18.3	4
IA	1,353	4.0	46.1	50.6	-4.5		48.5	48.2	0.3	7
ID	500	4.2	32.8	59.3	-26.6		27.6	67.2	-39.5	
IL	5,030	3.3	56.3	38.8	17.6	21	54.6	42.6	12.0	21
IN	2,564	3.7	45.7	51.7	-6.0		41.0	56.6	-15.6	
KS	1,148	4.6	39.2	56.1	-16.9		37.2	58.0	-20.8	
KY	1,645	3.7	41.7	55.1	-13.4		41.4	56.5	-15.1	
LA	2,030	3.6	48.2	49.2	-1.0		44.9	52.6	-7.7	
MA	2,772	4.1	60.2	32.2	28.0	12	59.8	32.5	27.3	12
MD	2,178	4.2	61.0	34.6	26.4	10	56.6	40.2	16.4	10
ME	677	4.0	47.3	42.3	5.0	4	49.1	44.0	5.1	4
MI	4,343	3.1	53.5	44.1	9.4	17	51.3	46.1	5.1	17
MN	2,376	3.7	45.4	48.7	-3.3		47.9	45.5	2.4	10
MO	2,659	3.4	49.3	47.6	1.7	11	47.1	50.4	-3.3	
MS	1,213	4.5	44.0	54.7	-10.6		40.7	57.6	-16.9	
MT	409	4.1	32.0	58.9	-26.9		33.4	58.4	-25.1	
NC	2,995	3.6	50.7	47.4	3.3	15	43.2	56.0	-12.8	
ND	313	4.1	31.9	63.2	-31.3		33.1	60.7	-27.6	
NE	710	3.8	29.7	64.9	-35.2		33.3	62.2	-29.0	
NH	571	3.6	47.2	47.5	-0.3		46.8	48.1	-1.3	
NJ	3,374	3.1	58.8	36.1	22.7	15	56.1	40.3	15.8	15
NM	647	4.3	49.0	45.1	3.8	5	47.9	47.8	0.1	5
NV	641	4.0	49.0	46.7	2.3	5	46.0	49.5	-3.5	
NY	7,004	2.6	59.2	33.9	25.3	31	60.2	35.2	25.0	31
OH	4,823	2.9	47.4	48.5	-1.1		46.5	50.0	-3.5	
OK	1,431	4.6	32.1	65.9	-33.8		38.4	60.3	-21.9	
OR	1,529	4.0	47.0	46.5	0.4	7	47.0	46.5	0.4	7
PA	4,988	3.0	51.1	45.3	5.8	21	50.6	46.4	4.2	21
RI	438	3.6	57.9	30.3	27.7	4	61.0	31.9	29.1	4
SC	1,725	4.4	45.6	51.6	-6.0		40.9	56.8	-15.9	
SD	311	5.1	35.3	63.1	-27.8		37.6	60.3	-22.7	
TN	2,183	3.9	54.4	43.5	10.9	11	47.3	51.1	-3.9	
TX	7,005	4.4	49.5	45.3	4.2	34	38.0	59.3	-21.3	
UT	829	3.8	23.2	70.1	-46.9		26.3	66.8	-40.5	
VA	2,962	3.2	48.6	47.9	0.6	13	44.4	52.5	-8.0	
VT	290	3.7	50.6	41.2	9.5	3	50.6	40.7	9.9	3
WA	2,527	3.0	52.5	40.3	12.1	11	50.1	44.6	5.6	11
WI	2,632	3.8	47.4	47.2	0.2	10	47.8	47.6	0.2	10
WV	732	4.5	43.9	52.4	-8.5		45.6	51.9	-6.3	
WY	219	4.3	28.2	66.9	-38.7		27.7	67.8	-40.1	

APPENDIX E: 2008 True Vote Sensitivity

2008 Turnout	Voted	Mix	Obama	McCain	Other
-	16.21	12.2%	71%	27%	2%
97%	62.43	47.0%	89%	9%	2%
97%	52.88	39.9%	17%	82%	1%
97%	1.17	0.88%	72%	26%	2%
116.5	132.70	100%	58.0%	40.4%	1.6%
	Cast	132.70	76.91	53.66	2.13
		Recorded	52.9%	45.6%	1.5%
		131.37	69.46	59.94	1.98

Obama % Of New		Obama % of Bush			
	15	16	17	18	19
		Obama % Share			
73	57.4	57.8	58.2	58.6	59.0
72	57.3	57.7	58.1	58.5	58.9
71	57.2	57.6	58.0	58.4	58.8
70	57.0	57.4	57.8	58.2	58.6
69	56.9	57.3	57.7	58.1	58.5
		Margin (millions)			
73	21.8	22.8	23.9	25.0	26.0
72	21.5	22.5	23.6	24.6	25.7
71	21.1	22.2	23.2	24.3	25.4
70	20.8	21.9	22.9	24.0	25.0
69	20.5	21.5	22.6	23.7	24.7

Bush % Turnout		Kerry % Turnout			
	95	96	97	98	99
		Obama % Share			
95	58.2	58.3	58.4	58.5	58.6
96	58.0	58.1	58.2	58.3	58.4
97	57.8	57.9	58.0	58.0	58.1
98	57.6	57.6	57.7	57.8	57.9
99	57.3	57.4	57.5	57.6	57.7
		Margin (millions)			
95	24.0	24.2	24.4	24.7	24.9
96	23.4	23.6	23.8	24.1	24.3
97	22.8	23.0	23.2	23.5	23.7
98	22.2	22.4	22.7	22.9	23.1
99	21.6	21.8	22.1	22.3	22.5

APPENDIX F: 2012 Election Model

Latest Poll Date: 10/24/2012
Assumptions:
50% Obama undecided voter allocation
3% margin of error
Returning voters based on 2008 Exit Poll

Obama needs 54-55% to overcome the fraud factor

True Vote Model	Obama	Romney
National Aggregate Projection	54.5	45.5
Popular Vote Win Probability	99.9	0.1
Electoral Vote Snapshot	371	167
Theoretical Expected EV	358.1	179.9

State Monte Carlo Simulation		
Aggregate Poll Share	48.4	45.8
Projected Share	51.3	48.7
Popular Vote Win Prob	81.0	19.0
Electoral Vote Win Prob	94.8	5.2
Electoral Vote Snapshot	301	237
Electoral Vote Simulation	301.1	236.9
Theoretical Expected EV	302.1	235.9
Maximum trial EV	352	186
Minimum trial EV	241	297

National Polls		
Average	47.2	47.9
Projected Share	49.7	50.4
Popular Vote Win Prob	36.6	63.4
Gallup LV Tracking	45	51
Rasmussen LV Tracking	46	50

18 Battleground states (205 EV)

Obama leads in 14 (138 EV)	50.4	47.6

APPENDIX G: 2010 Midterms

Florida	Gov.	Unadjusted Exit Poll			Adjusted Exit Poll (recorded)			
2008	Mix	Sink	Scott	Other	Mix	Sink	Scott	Other
Obama	47%	90%	8%	2%	47%	88%	10%	2%
McCain	47%	11%	85%	4%	47%	11%	87%	2%
Other	3%	54%	30%	16%	3%	32%	66%	2%
DNV	3%	55%	30%	15%	3%	31%	67%	2%
Share	100%	50.7%	45.5%	3.8%	100%	48.4%	49.6%	2.0%
Votes	5282	2680	2404	198	5282	2557	2619	106

Exit Poll Respondent	3156	1600	1437	119
		50.7%	45.5%	3.8%

Ohio Gov.

2008	Mix	Unadjusted Exit Poll			Adjusted Exit Poll (recorded)			
		Strickland	Kasich	Other	Mix	Strickland	Kasich	Other
Obama	45%	86%	12%	2%	45%	83%	14%	3%
		15%	83%			15%	83%	2%
McCain	47%			2%	47%			
Other	3%	52%	36%	12%	3%	42%	57%	1%
DNV	5%	53%	36%	11%	5%	42%	56%	2%
Share	100%	50.0%	47.3%	2.7%	100%	47.8%	49.8%	2.4%
Votes	3,795	1896	1795	104	3795	1812	1891	92

Exit Poll Respondents	3305	49.9%	47.4%	2.7%
		1649	1565	91

Illinois Senate

2008	Mix	Unadjusted Exit Poll		Adjusted Exit Poll (recorded)		
		Giannoulias	Kirk	Mix	Giannoulias	Kirk
Obama	57%	83%	15%	56.3%	79%	18%
McCain	38%	3%	95%	38.4%	3%	93%
Other	1%	52%	48%	1.3%	50%	50%
DNV	4%	50%	49%	4.0%	30%	70%
Total	100%	51.0%	47.1%	100%	47.5%	49.3%
Exit Poll	2325	1187	1094	3616	1720	1779

APPENDIX H: Walker Recall True Vote Model

2008	Vote	Mix	Barrett	Walker	Trivedi
Obama	1,350,669	53.7%	90.0%	9.4%	0.6%
McCain	1,016,934	40.4%	7.0%	92.4%	0.6%
Other	35,239	1.4%	50.0%	49.4%	0.6%
DNV	113,223	4.5%	56.2%	43.2%	0.6%
Total	2,516,065	100%	54.4%	45.1%	0.6%
			1,368,097	1,133,505	14,463
84.60%	Turnout				
		Recd	46.3%	53.1%	0.6%
		Vote	1,164,480	1,335,585	14,463

	Barrett share of Obama voters		
Barrett	88%	90%	92%
%McCain	Barrett	Share	
9%	54.1%	55.2%	56.3%
7%	53.3%	54.4%	55.4%
5%	52.5%	53.6%	54.6%
	Barrett	Margin	
9%	221,243	275,270	329,297
7%	180,566	234,593	288,619
5%	1,398	193,915	247,942

	Returning Obama voter turnout		
McCain	73%	83%	97%
Turnout	Barrett	Share	
73%	54.6%	57.2%	59.8%
83%	51.8%	54.9%	56.9%
97%	49.0%	54.4%	54.1%
	Barrett	Margin	
73%	247,080	376,533	505,985
83%	105,140	364,045	364,045
97%	-36,800	92,653	222,105

Wisconsin State Senate Recalls

District	2008 Obama	2008 McCain	2011 Senate Recorded Vote Dem	2011 Senate Recorded Vote GOP	2011 Senate Recorded Vote Margin
2	52.4%	46.2%	42.6%	57.4	-14.8%
8	51.5%	47.5%	46.3%	53.7%	-7.3%
10	50.3%	48.0%	42.3%	57.7%	-15.3%
14	51.9%	46.8%	47.8%	52.2%	-4.3%
18	51.4%	47.4%	51.1%	48.9%	2.3%
32	60.9%	37.7%	55.4%	44.6%	10.8%
All	53.0%	45.7%	47.6%	52.4%	-4.8%
12	52.8%	45.8%	54.1%	45.9%	8.2%
22	57.3%	41.4%	57.6%	42.4%	15.1%
30	56.6%	42.2%	66.6%	33.4%	33.2%
All	55.5%	43.2%	58.8%	41.2%	17.6%

Turnout Required to Match the Recorded Vote

District	Zero Net Defection Obama Turnout	Zero Net Defection McCain Turnout	Zero Net Defection Total Turnout	Repubs win 95% of McCain Turnout	Repubs win 95% of McCain Dem % of Obama
2	40%	64%	51%	63%	76%
8	64%	81%	72%	79%	84%
10	52%	76%	63%	68%	78%
14	56%	68%	62%	82%	86%
18	63%	65%	64%	97%	94%
32	61%	76%	67%	80%	87%
All	58%	74%	63%	78%	85%
12	51%	49%	50%	104%	97%
22	52%	52%	52%	100%	96%
30	49%	31%	41%	158%	98%
All	51%	45%	48%	113%	98%

APPENDIX I: Margin of Error Table

N= number of poll respondents
S= winning 2-party poll share
C= Cluster effect (exit poll)

MoE = Margin of error = $(1+C) * 1.96 * \sqrt{S * (1-S) / N}$

Win Probability = NORMDIST(S, .5, MoE/1.96, true)

The confidence level (probability) is 95% that the population mean
is within the range: S - MoE < S < S + MoE

	2-party winning exit poll share				
N	50	53	55	60	70

Exit Poll Margin of Error
(30% cluster effect)

N	50	53	55	60	70
500	5.70	5.69	5.67	5.58	5.22
1,000	4.03	4.02	4.01	3.95	3.69
1,500	3.29	3.28	3.27	3.22	3.01
2,000	2.85	2.84	2.83	2.79	2.61
3,000	2.33	2.32	2.31	2.28	2.13
10,000	1.27	1.27	1.27	1.25	1.17
13,660	1.09	1.09	1.08	1.07	1.00
17,836	0.95	0.95	0.95	0.93	0.87

Win Probability

N	50	53	55	60	70
500	50	84.9	95.8	99.98	100
1,000	50	92.8	99.3	100	100
1,500	50	96.3	99.9		
2,000	50	98.1	99.97		
3,000	50	99.4	100		
10,000	50	100			
13,660	50				
17,836	50				

ACKNOWLEDGMENTS

This book is dedicated to my wife Maia and the Tampa General Hospital doctors and nurses who saved my life in 2006.

And to the Wisconsin citizens who have fought gallantly for election integrity along with Bob Fitrakis, Harvey Wasserman, Cliff Arnebeck, Mark Crispin Miller, Jonathan Simon, Greg Palast, Jesse Ventura, Dennis Kern, Michael Collins, Michael Carmichael, Robert F. Kennedy Jr., Michael Keefer, Ion Sancho, Kathy Dopp, Ron Baiman, Paul Lehto, Lynn Landes, Rebecca Mercuri, Lorraine Minnite, Steven F. Freeman, Bill Breitsprecher, David Griscom, Thom Hartmann, Brad Friedman, Victoria Collier, Sheila Parks, Jeannie Dean, Bev Harris ....and Bill Higham.

Last but not least, to my mother, who much to my surprise showed up one day in my algebra class. She came to speak with the teacher about my poor grades. It was a major turning point in my life. From then on, I began to take things seriously and always did my homework.

ABOUT THE AUTHOR

Richard Charnin holds a B.A. degree in Mathematics from Queens College (NY) and advanced degrees in Applied Mathematics (Adelphi University) and Operations Research (Polytechnic Institute of NY). His first position was a Numerical Control engineer/programmer with Grumman Aerospace Corporation, a major defense manufacturer of corporate and military aircraft and the Lunar Module.

In the mid 1970s, Charnin was hired as a manager/programmer of corporate financial/ investment banking division of Merrill Lynch White Weld Capital Markets. After ten years on Wall Street, he worked as an independent software developer consulting for financial, investment and industrial corporations. Applications included corporate financial planning, forecasting, mergers and acquisitions, securities valuation and investment analysis.

Posting as *Truth Is All* on various election discussion forums, he has applied his mathematical programming experience in developing election forecasting and post-election analytical models. The *2004 Election Model* was the first to use Monte Carlo simulation for calculating the probability of winning the electoral vote. The forecast closely matched the exit polls.

The *True Vote Model* was developed to address impossible anomalies in the 2004 national exit poll. The model has been confirmed by matching the unadjusted 1988-2008 state and national exit polls. It complements the massive evidence of systemic election fraud compiled by other election analysts.

In 2010 Charnin wrote *Proving Election Fraud: Phantom Voters, Uncounted Votes and the National Exit Poll.*